77 Ways to Energize Your Sunday School Class

77 Ways to Energize Your Sunday School Class

Judy Gattis Smith

Abingdon Press
Nashville

77 WAYS TO ENERGIZE YOUR SUNDAY SCHOOL CLASS

This book is printed on recycled, acid-free paper.

Library of Congress Cataloging-in-Publication Data

SMITH, JUDY GATTIS, 1933–
    77 ways to energize your Sunday school class   :   glimpsing God through colored windows /
Judy Gattis Smith.
        p.   cm.
    Includes index.
    ISBN 0-687-38114-2 (alk. paper)
    1. Christian education—Teaching methods.   I. Title.   II. Title: Seventy-seven ways to
energize your Sunday school class.
BV1534.S638   1991
268'.6—dc20   91-34040
                                                                                            CIP

Scripture quotations, except for brief paraphrases or unless otherwise noted, are from the New Revised Standard Version Bible, copyright © 1989, by the Division of Christian Education of the National Council of the Churches of Christ in the United States of America. Used by permission.

Those noted KJV are from the King James Version.

Those noted GNB are from the *Good News Bible*—Old Testament: Copyright © American Bible Society 1976; New Testament: Copyright © American Bible Society 1966, 1971, 1976.

Excerpts from "Jesu, Jesu," by Tom Colvin, pages 56–57, are copyright © 1969 by Hope Publishing Co., Carol Stream, IL 60188. All rights reserved. Used by permission.

MANUFACTURED IN THE UNITED STATES OF AMERICA

To my special Mary friends of many years:

Mary Allen Ingram,
Mary Lou Sewell,
and
Mary Jane Layne

In the creation of this book appreciation is due many people. First of all to my husband of thirty-six years, David Smith, who is my kite string. He keeps me from floating away with too many wild ideas. Thanks to Paul Franklyn and Jill Reddig, who have been supportive and encouraging editors and have given me a format in which to present my thoughts. Thanks to Steve Cox for his careful preparation of the manuscript. Thanks to the Christian Educators Fellowship of the Mississippi Conference United Methodist Church, who first tried these ideas out with me, and to the participants in a class at the Presbyterian School of Christian Education, Richmond, Virginia, who worked through the completed book with me. Thanks also to the many church school teachers and Christian educators around the country who shared helpful ideas and insights.

CONTENTS

CREATIVITY IN THE SUNDAY SCHOOL CLASS

It is time to seek the Lord,
*   that he may come and rain righteousness upon you.*
*   —Hosea 10:12*

See if I will not open the windows of heaven for you and pour
down for you an overflowing blessing.
*   —Malachi 3:10*

Dictionary definition
SEEK: *to look for*

INTRODUCTION

Ann Weems in her poem "Good News Music" asks: "How long will we come before the Lord with tired spirits and droning voices?" We add, "How long will 'boring' be an adjective describing Sunday school?" The work we are given to do as Sunday school teachers is exciting, meaningful, and important, not "ho hum." Sometimes our denominational curriculum alone does not kindle this excitement we seek. We must supplement it. We are challenged to bring our creative best to this task.

Are you now, or would you like in the future to be described as a creative Sunday school teacher? This book is to affirm that that is just what you are. Some people think creativity is a talent or personality trait, but creativity is not a special gift. It is a normal and necessary part of everyone's thinking. You are creative because you are unique. There is no one else in all the world just like you. At its core, teaching is a creative act. No one will teach a class in just the way you teach it, because the lesson is filtered through your unique life and experiences. Teaching at your creative best will excite and interest students so much that they will keep coming back for more.

I saw a banner in a church that read: "You can't beat God for creativity." We start here, with the fact that we believe we are made in the image of a Creator God who *did* create and *is* creating and *will* create and re-create forever. We (the reflected image of this God) can learn to release more of the creativity within us. We can learn to affirm and use our special avenues of creativity. This book seeks to open up the fun of creative approaches for beginning teachers who struggle to master techniques and procedures. It is also to enliven experienced teachers who may have become dulled with familiar routines. We seek to free teachers from ingrained rituals of teaching and to demonstrate teaching as the glorious

experience of being alive and curious. As long as you and your students are alive and curious your classroom will not be boring.

> We think of creativity as free-flowing, unstructured, disencumbered, but creative teaching is like playing a game; it has certain important rules:
> **1.** There is no one way to teach a class.
> **2.** There is no one correct way to learn.
> **3.** The status quo can always be adjusted.
> **4.** Final solutions are always tentative.
> **5.** Rejection or ridicule of ideas or persons is unacceptable.
> **6.** Mistakes are acceptable.

First, we will look at the whole field of creativity as it applies to us as church school teachers. We'll consider "Why bother being creative?" Next we'll explore "Where do you get your ideas?" and introduce an approach to creativity using the image of colored windows.

In the second part of this book, we'll seek to put our creativity to work. Dozens of specific ideas are suggested for your creative use in your classroom.

Questions about God, about how people behave toward one another, and about how to live are some of the big questions people ask themselves during their lives. Answers are drawn from many sources and all kinds of learning. Surely one of our greatest inheritances is the ability to learn, but the ways we learn are different. The excitement of a colored-window approach to teaching is that it accommodates the diversity we are now finding in our classrooms.

For convenience, we will divide the ways we learn into four specific categories. For clarification we will use the metaphor of the colored window. We affirm that each of these four ways of learning is good, and that a gifted teacher can apparently make almost any style of instruction work. This book affirms that learning can best take place when we discover our unique creativity and that of our class and offer this in service to God.

It is my hope that your creative potential will be brought to the forefront, polished up, and renewed; that you will have confidence to try some new things, the courage to fail and go on to something else; that you will see new depths to your own creativity; and that your experience of teaching will be enriched and enlivened.

WHY BOTHER BEING CREATIVE?

Being creative to keep boredom out of the classroom is not its only benefit. We bother about being creative for at least two other reasons:

1. Because we live in a world of change and flux. When circumstances change it is no longer possible to solve today's problems with yesterday's solutions. What worked in the church even five years ago won't work today. We can bemoan this fact or we can look for new answers, solutions, and ideas. This calls for a flexibility and spontaneity in ourselves as teachers. We become as sensitive as possible to our students' own immediate experiences, to what they think and feel and believe now, to where they are hurting, to current sources of pain. The truths we have to teach are eternal, but our methods can be as up-to-date as this morning's newspaper. We can find inspiration in the words of Isaiah 43:19 (GNB): "Watch for the new thing I am going to do. It is happening already—you can see it now." And we watch eagerly for its unfolding.

2. We bother about being creative because it is good for us! My interest was piqued while reading a book review of *Mindfulness*, by Ellen Langer, professor of psychology at Harvard (Addison-Wesley, 1989). According to this review, the book states that the kindest way to care for the elderly is to make life a little less comfortable, less predictable, more demanding. Out of well-intended protectiveness, we've created for many elderly people a world without challenges, without surprises, without uncertainty. But that world isn't soothing, it's deadening. Langer's research suggests that many elderly people are dying prematurely simply as a result of mental stagnation. Langer encouraged a group of nursing and retirement home residents to take part in a 20-minute "mental workout" every morning and afternoon. The session involved such activities as dreaming up new uses for everyday objects. After three weeks the elderly subjects' blood pressures were lower and they felt younger, happier, and more in control of their lives. Even more remarkably they also lived longer. Langer reports that at follow-up three years later 87.5 percent of the experimental group was still alive, versus 62.5 percent of the baseline group.

What was crucial, says Langer, were the mental processes sparked. The workouts were designed to force the subjects to view the old and familiar in a new light. "Mindful people live in a world of possibilities. Contrary to popular belief, mindlessness isn't relaxing, it's debilitating. And mindfulness isn't exhausting, it's enlivening."

If this works in nursing homes why not in our Sunday school classes? If it works for the elderly, why not for all ages? We can focus on solving the problems of our day with our unique gifts. We can stretch our minds to new solutions and assimilate and use new experiences. We can take a creative approach to Sunday school teaching that deals with new ideas and new ways of looking at things.

> Jerusalem, go up on a high mountain,
>   and proclaim the good news!
> Call out with a loud voice, Zion;
>   announce the good news!
> Speak out and do not be afraid.
> Tell the towns of Judah
>   that their God is coming!
>   —Isaiah 40:9 GNB

And tell that news in as enlivened and creative a way as you can!

Where do creative ideas come from? How do we get the creative juices flowing? Ideas are everywhere, all the time. Most of the time though, we simply don't notice they are there.

It's like radio waves. We are told that radio waves travel around us constantly, but we don't hear them unless we have a receiver. Radios are made to pick up radio signals, but even they can't do it if their power isn't turned on. We are like that. Our brains are made to pick up idea signals, but how can we turn on the power to do so?

Our uniqueness comes into play again. Different people pick up creative ideas in different ways. Our own experiences and observations give our imaginations material to work with.

Take a moment now. Stop reading and reflect on where you get your creative ideas. What motivates you to be creative? Ask yourself this question: When was the last time I came up with a really great creative idea for my Sunday school class? What was it? Where did the idea come from?

Following are eight ways some teachers have been stimulated to create new ideas. Is your way included in this list?

1. *Brainstorming.* An old standby in Christian education is still a reliable source of creative ideas—brainstorming (coming up with everything you can think of on a given subject).

Gather a group, such as your class or a group of teachers, together and ask them to toss off ideas from the top of their heads, without deliberate thought or meditation, on a given topic. Write down the ideas quickly. Do not stop and discuss any idea, just write and think quickly and spontaneously. There is something that happens in a group using this method. An idea you hear suggests another to you and a chain reaction of popping ideas is set off. Encourage the group to be very free. Crazy, absurd, illogical ideas can evoke a response from another. Accept every idea presented and write it down no matter how insignificant or even silly. It may be the spark for a usable idea.

This method seems to counteract a danger we often face in Christian education where someone offers one idea and then the discussion stops. We seem to get stuck with that one idea. I once heard a children's sermon where the leader held up a fairystone (those unique formations in the shape of tiny crosses). "What is this?" the leader asked. "A rock," one boy replied, and then, it was as if thinking stopped. The children were not able to see anything beyond a rock. We need to ask, "What are the answers," not "What is *the* answer?" if we are seeking creativity in our thinking. Receiving an answer, we can reply, "That's good. What are some more?"

An intriguing proverb says: "Nothing is as dangerous as an idea when it is the only one you have." Brainstorming has the advantage of allowing us to give more than one answer to a question, and creative ideas are often born here.

Recently I asked a group of Christian educators to brainstorm the question, "How can we get more Sunday school teachers?" I have struggled with that question for many years in many church settings and tried as hard as I could to find solutions.

The brainstorming started slowly and with traditional answers but grew wilder and freer. (With this method an astronomical number of possible patterns can emerge.) When we had exhausted our thoughts on the subject we looked at our long list and circled those that might possibly work in our setting. From the profusion of ideas could we extract a gem for personal use? An idea I had never thought of struck me as right for my current church situation: "Offer the teachers free parking places on Sunday morning."

A strange idea but one that met some problems and needs we faced and one I am sure I would never have thought of alone.

Creative ideas are often born in brainstorming.

2. *Metaphors.* One of the most fertile powers we as humans possess is that of comparing one thing to something else. If we are faced with a problem and can make a metaphor of it we get a fresh slant. We see the problem from another angle. It is easier for some people than for others to think in metaphors.

A Christian educator told me that she does most of her problem solving through metaphors, and she shared this story with me:

The education committee of her church had just learned that their pastor was being transferred. This had a devastating effect on the committee because this minister had been the spearhead of their activities and their leader in setting a new educational direction for the church. What would happen now? How could they possibly continue?

The meeting of the committee went in circles for more than an hour. Then it ended in depression. In solemnity the group assembled at a local restaurant for lunch.

As they were eating one of the members pointed to a picture on the wall of the restaurant.

"Look!" she said.

The picture was of a tree stump. It was obvious the tree had been cut down some time before and the upper part completely removed. But growing out of the dead-looking stump was a tiny green sprout.

"Yes" the group responded, making the connection in their minds between the picture and their situation.

Applying the metaphor idea to your teaching situation, think of your class. Can you compare your class or your teaching to a fruit and come up with a new way of looking at your students and your situations?

For example, one teacher said: "My teaching is like eating an apple. Sometimes I take it like it is and just enjoy it. Sometimes I follow a recipe and cook up something different." Another said: "My class is like a bunch of bananas. Some are green and unripe. Some are soft and mushy." Still another said: "My class is like an orange. I have to remove a lot of peel to get to the fruit." Another added: "My class is like an onion. They come on too strong."

Christian educators of Delaware's Peninsula Conference of The United Methodist Church chose a metaphor as their theme one year: *To Grow a Teacher: Vine and Branches.* Their strategy included "A New Green Shoot," "Growing Toward the Sun," and "Productive Harvest." The metaphor creates mind pictures; it enhances creativity.

3. *Ask "What If?"* Asking the question "What if?" is a source of creative ideas for many people. It gives them the freedom to think differently. It opens up fascinating situations and answers.

Ask yourself or your class, "What if there were no Sunday school?" "How would this affect our church?" "Where would we learn about our faith and religious traditions?" "What things would be different if there were no Sunday school?"

"What if . . . ?"

Or, ask "What if we had no curriculum materials?" "Where would we start?" "How would we know where to begin in teaching about our faith?" It has been my experience that youth classes in particular are often unhappy with their denominational Sunday school material. This is a good "What if?" question to ask them and could lead to some interesting new avenues of study.

Or, "What if no one had written down the Bible? Would we have a church?"

Almost every Bible story can reveal new layers of meaning if we ask the question "What if?"

"What if the boy with the loaves and the fishes had not shared his food? Would Jesus have been able to perform a miracle?" "What if Jesus had not been crucified but lived to an old age, continuing to teach? What would have been the consequences? How would the church be different?"

Creative teaching is imagining the possibilities.

4. *Another Area of Study.* Looking in a whole other area of study can be a source for creative ideas. Consider this statement by Peter Borden, a scientist: "Most advances in science come when a person for one reason or another is forced to change fields."

What is your particular hobby or interest right now? Could this be brought into your classroom teaching?

Once I had the privilege of co-teaching a Junior High class with a gifted artist. Using his talents we taught the whole year through art media. We made a book of linoleum block prints to teach a unit on Jesus' miracles. Through paper sculpture we taught a unit on how the Bible came to be.

I know a sixth-grade teacher who is a gifted seamstress. Her class studied the history of United Methodism by making a quilt of historical events and places.

Music could be used as a medium for teaching, as could gardening . . . reading . . . sports. Consider what really interests you and try to find the connection between this field and your Sunday school teaching. Look for analogous situations. You are not using your interests to provide recreation for your class but as a source of creative ideas. Great ideas are lying in a field close to yours. We cross-fertilize ideas for creativity.

We look in new fields, sometimes unusual outside places, because we never know when these ideas might come together to form a new creative approach.

5. *Do It Differently.* Take something you do in a traditional way and do it differently. Does your Sunday school class start the same way every time? Some adult classes always begin with a hymn, an opening devotion, announcements, and offerings. Ask "Why did we start doing this? When did it start? Who started it? Do these reasons for doing it this way still exist?"

We do not want to have change just for change's sake, but changing a traditional format often opens up creative approaches. Remember the rule: The status quo is always adjustable.

Changing from a traditional time frame can also foster creative new approaches. Some churches have asked, "What time frame other than Sunday morning could work for Sunday school?" with good results.

The new format of creating an environment for Vacation Bible School like a New Testament village or an Old Testament oasis has opened up many creative responses to the traditional Vacation Bible School setting.

Using this approach, ask the question "How many ways can this be done?" and see what you come up with.

A creative teacher is willing to look for alternatives.

6. *Failure.* Failure is a great source of creative ideas. We learn quickly what doesn't work and we are given the opportunity to try new approaches. We have to take risks in our teaching and sometimes these risks end in failure.

I often ask, in my workshops, "Is there anyone here who has never failed?" I am all prepared to say, "Don't worry, you will," but, so far, I have not encountered any teacher who hasn't failed at some time. A disastrous class forces us to ask, "What went wrong? What should I be doing differently?"

If we are serious in trying to be creative teachers we find that the same energy which generates good, creative ideas also produces failures.

We don't like failure, because it is painful. It points out our weaknesses. Among the many evils of drugs is they allow us to continue to fail without pain. They numb us. We must accept the fact that pain usually accompanies failure and move creatively from there. Creative ideas are often born out of discomfort.

Occasionally we find a child in our class who is reluctant to try any approach that could lead to failure. This is the child who constantly checks with you to see if she is doing it "right." We might even recognize this tendency in ourselves.

I have often found great comfort in the Bible passage II Corinthians 12:9 (KJV): "My grace is sufficient for thee: for my strength is made perfect in weakness."

How can we teach grace if we are always perfect? We may sometimes be afraid that we will do or say something foolish, or we may fear that our new ideas will make our old ideas seem foolish. No one enjoys being wrong. Rather than gloomy failure think of it as playful willingness to take risks. Go ahead and try your new, crazy, creative idea. As one wag said, "In the church it is easier to ask forgiveness than permission."

Another possibility is that your "failure" may just be an idea whose time has not come. You may be doing something that seems ridiculous or useless to the people around you. Your idea may not be appreciated until many years later. Remember that when Igor Stravinsky introduced *The Rite of Spring* in 1913, people thought they had been insulted, believing Stravinsky was trying to get them to accept noise as music. It turned out to be the beginning of an entirely new kind of music. Your failure may simply be telling you that you are a person ahead of your time.

7. *What Others Have Done.* Being a creative Sunday school teacher doesn't mean you are completely novel. What has worked for other teachers and in other churches may be just the creative spark you need. This is one of the greatest benefits of our national conferences and workshops with other churches and denominations. This is why we subscribe to Christian education magazines and publications. We are constantly on the lookout for interesting ideas that have worked for others.

It seems to be generally true that ideas are best in the church if they are not *too* new, if in some way they are seen as similar to old and tried ideas that are known to work.

I vividly remember the first time we used creative movement in a worship service. I was fearful of how it would be received by some older members of our congregation, but following the service an elderly woman came up to me and said, "That was just like we used to do in elocution class." From then on I introduced movement to older church members by comparing it to elocution classes.

No ideas are really new, but they are creative and unique if we adapt them to our situation and if we relate them to the particular needs, interests, and abilities of our students. By taking what we know and putting it together in new ways we are being creative teachers.

8. *Humor.* Humor can be a source of creative ideas. Humor often involves looking at something in a different way. The incongruity between one way of thinking and another produces humor.

I was told of a caption placed over the church nursery in a church in Kentucky that uses a verse from Colossians in an entirely new context. The verse reads, "We may not all sleep but we shall all be changed."

Appreciating this humor requires seeing two contradictory notions at the same time, and this is the same skill needed for creative thinking.

Kirk Mariner, a United Methodist minister in the Virginia Conference, is known for his creativity. He tells of using humor as a creative technique in his children's sermons. One morning, as the children assembled in the front of the church, he displayed a large poster with the words from John 3:16, some of them omitted. In place of the omissions, he superimposed words in parentheses for comic effect:

God so loved _____

(only girls) (only good people) (only people)

that he gave _____

(a lot of money) (a special gift)

that_____
(all adults) (Americans)

should not perish but have _____.
(good health) (a lot of fun)

Again, seeing familiar words in a new context produced the creative spark.

These are only a few of the methods that can be used to stimulate creativity. Deadlines and schedules push some people's creative buttons.

Some persons like to go to crowded areas like shopping malls and observe people. What are they doing? What interesting things are going on? What do we see that tells us of our particular time? What do store windows tell us? Ideas come from outside. From everything we see and do.

Others are most creative when they are alone and allow their minds to daydream. Fantasies, images, castle-building, illusions are their tools. Their ideas come from inside when their own imagination starts mixing with the outside.

Still others search their memories and ponder the experiences of their lives. What from my past could help me interpret this situation? They search for remembered incidents or sensations. They keep journals and jot down their thoughts and insights. A word filtered through the sieve of their unique consciousness allows them to create.

Travel and books are also sources of creative ideas for some persons. Add these personality traits: receptivity, an intuitive sense, sensuousness, openness, a delight in juxtaposing and savoring incongruous ideas and constant wonder.

Where do *you* get *your* creative ideas? Is your source one of the ones mentioned above or would you add even more possibilities?

Creativity is a state of mind ready to turn any stimulus into an idea. That idea is like a grain of sand. It's just there and we are not sure what will become of it. Creative teachers are like oysters. That idea is the grain of sand in the oyster shell. It worries us and bothers us and causes us to put forth extra effort. And then, if we are lucky, we create a pearl.

Sometimes we are afraid to use our imaginations simply because we aren't used to doing it. We are as rusty as the Tin Man in the *Wizard of Oz* and as stiff and inflexible. It is always more comfortable to act and think as we have before.

But opening up your own unique style of creativity is exciting, as you think about something you have never thought about before, and fun, as you share that idea with your class and they begin to feel excited too.

A sensitive Sunday school teacher never ceases to wonder at the mystery and marvel of inflowing power that comes, all undeserving, from God's gracious love. When we tap into a creative idea we have a tiny glimpse of our Creator God.

FOUR APPROACHES TO CREATIVE TEACHING

There is an old folktale with many versions that tells of a small boy who visits an ancient relative. This relative always gives him something to carry home to his mother. The boy never quite understands how to carry the object he has been given. When the relative gives him cake, he squeezes it tightly in his hands to safely preserve it. On arriving home he opens his hands to find only crumbs. His mother informs him that he should have wrapped the cake and put it under his hat on his head. The next gift from the elderly relative is sweet, freshly churned butter. The boy follows the previous instructions and arrives home with melted butter dripping down his face. Whereupon the mother instructs him to carry butter wrapped in nice green leaves and to stop along the way to dip it in the cool creek. Next the relative gives the boy a puppy, which he proceeds to wrap in leaves and dip in the creek. The story goes on and on with the boy carefully following instructions but never quite grasping what it is he is supposed to do.

Have you ever felt like this in teaching Sunday school? You follow instructions and lesson plans, but you vaguely suspect that you have gotten something wrong. Something has been left out. Somehow it did not quite go right. The results are not what was expected. And so you drift and waffle and react rather than teach purposefully.

These are not unusual feelings when we realize that teaching in Sunday school is different from any other kind of teaching. How do we teach so that our students will have a personal relationship with the living God? What lesson plan ensures that students will understand that the Bible is a history book *and* an inspired book that speaks to the present *and* the future? What methods capture the experience of the Holy Spirit? What obtainable goal can be reached in teaching the meaning of life? How do we evaluate increased sensitivity?

Henry Ward Beecher once said, "If you can think it out, that is your privilege. If you feel it out, that is your privilege. Wherever you have seen God pass, mark it and go and sit in that window again." Dr. Beecher's statement provides us with some answers to our questions above.

1. There is more than one way to catch a glimpse of God.

2. If we know what window we are looking out of, we can see more clearly. We will bring to the window a certain perspective. It makes us aware of what we are teaching and learning.

3. By using categories we can organize our thinking. Organizing our thinking and learning can lead us to a new way of perceiving what it is we do.

The quotation from Dr. Beecher offers a stimulating idea. There are several windows to creativity that are available in the Sunday school.

Imagine a large room. In this room are four large windows. One windowframe is painted white. One windowframe is painted indigo. Around the third window is the color red, and encircling the fourth window is the color yellow. The room is your classroom, and the four windows are four approaches you will take with your class, four windows through which you and your students will look for a glimpse of God.

- The white window is the window of factual thinking.
- The indigo window is the window of negative thinking.
- The red window is the window of feelings.
- The yellow window is the window of visions and dreams.

How will using these window images help us in teaching? The technique will clarify just what it is we are doing.

When large corporations perceive their work as stale, flat, and unprofitable, they seek to understand why and proceed to make changes. I read with interest the way Edward De Bono, an authority in the field of conceptual thinking, worked with such groups as IBM, Exxon, Procter and Gamble, Bell Telephone, DuPont, and others to categorize their working techniques for efficiency and productivity (*Six Thinking Hats,* Little, Brown and Co., 1986). As I read I wondered: Is there not something here for those of us in the church? Something that would help us do our job better and give us more satisfaction in our work?

Our work in the church is in a dimension different from that of industry of course. The church is not a corporation but a special fellowship with a unique mission. Yet we work through a systematic structure. Improving and fine-tuning the structure could be helpful. The colored windows suggest our categories.

By clearly understanding which window we are looking out of, we are able to focus our thinking more clearly, generate more creative ideas. It helps us immensely in the difficult task of communicating with one another. Many times in our teaching, confusion arises because we try to do too much at once. Feelings and emotions, dreams and logic all crowd in on us (and with usually only about 45 minutes on Sunday morning to cover them all!).

The remainder of this book seeks to help by allowing us to do one thing at a time. We separate, for learning purposes, emotions from logic, visions from doubts. Looking out a special window defines a certain type of learning. Each of the following chapters deals with one of the four windows and suggests at least two dozen specific activities or experiences you and your class can engage in. If we compartmentalize our teaching so that we better understand what we are attempting to do, we can choose methods to accomplish our goals and feel secure in our choices.

The colors chosen for the windows help us to visualize them and are related to their function.

White is the absence of color, therefore neutral and objective. Looking out the white window we will deal with facts and figures separated from feelings, for, in teaching the faith, there are facts to be learned.

Indigo is a dark grayish blue and suggests neutrality. Looking out the indigo window we deal with negative facts and doubts. Our first impression may be that this is something to avoid in Sunday school teaching, but hopefully you will discover many advantages to studying negative aspects.

Red suggests emotions and feelings, from fire to blood to valentines. Looking out the red window we use the lens of feelings to focus our glimpse of God.

Yellow suggests the sun and positive emotions and energy. Looking through the yellow window we use visions and dreams in order to show us God.

Pause for a moment in your reading now. Picture your Sunday school class vividly in your mind. Write down in the space at the top of page 22 your desired outcomes of a year of Sunday school. Let your mind wander and dream. What would you like to see happen? What results do you desire?

Look at your list. Color code the items according to the learning windows. Is there a certain body of factual information you would like your class to learn this year? Leave it white. Would you like to resolve some problems in your class? Mark these indigo. Does your list include words such as "prejudice," or "enthusiasm" or "joy" or "pain"? Mark these red. Is there a mission statement on your list, or a vocational emphasis, or a search for guidance or direction? Mark it yellow.

Now by compartmentalizing our thoughts we have a better handle on how to deal with them. We learn which methods work best for each window. We understand what we are trying to do and we can focus now on the most creative way to do it.

We can explain the window images to our class, which will clarify learning for them, too. For example, after explaining the concept to your class you might say, "Today we are looking out the white window. We are searching just for facts." "Let's take this parable of Jesus and use the red window outlook. What feelings does it arouse in you?" "Imagine you are looking out the yellow window as you say over and over these words from the Psalmist. Is God speaking a special word to you?" "This saying of Jesus seems to turn everything upside down. Look out the indigo window for a moment. What are some negative results of this saying? Who is Jesus making angry? What is going to happen?"

This approach is also a great antidote for the student who is always negative. We might say to such a student: "We are not using the indigo window outlook right now."

The window image serves as a signaling device to your class. It indicates a certain type of learning, that we are trying to think in a certain manner.

Teaching, of course, can never be rigidly kept in compartments. We will not be using a certain window outlook at every teaching moment, but using the image of the colored window can help us unscramble thinking so that we are not trying to cover everything at once. Instead of wasting time in arguments and drifting discussions, we will have a more disciplined approach. Compartmentalizing magnifies a part of the whole.

To reiterate its advantages, compartmentalizing our thinking and learning:

1. directs our attention where we need to direct it.
2. is a convenient way of asking someone to shift gears.
3. focuses our thinking more clearly.
4. improves communication.

In a way this window approach is a variation of the old theme of styles of learning that we have studied about in Christian education for many years. The difference is that we are making a deliberate attempt to recognize the various styles, to name them, and to categorize. It almost makes a game out of staying strictly within the borders of one style of learning for a given period of time and for a given purpose. In addition it adds the yellow window of visions and dreams, not usually included in styles of learning. There is often an imbalance in our traditional curriculum that ignores the inner world of visions and dreams, that omits this way of knowing.

We now explore these four ways (windows) to search for God and methods to facilitate the searching. For Christian educators and Sunday school teachers, the examples under "Ideas" are to acquaint you with the *type* of methods that work best with each window. When you feel secure with the type of methods suggested for each window, try devising your own ideas, using your creative gifts.

The Bible verse "Love the Lord with *all* your heart and soul and mind" accompanies each window section to remind us that the best alternative to boredom is enthusiasm and the best prod to creativity is deep love of what we are doing.

IDEAS FOR ALL AGES

There are certain items of information that educators tell us can best be learned at definite ages. Just what *facts* do we want our students to learn as they progress through the Sunday school? The answer is found in White Window learning. So, under the White Window section of the Table of Contents, facts appropriate to each age level are given. One or more suggestive, creative ideas, also appropriate to the age level, follow. Suggestions are given for *every* age level in the Sunday school.

Red Window feelings, Indigo Window doubts, and Yellow Window visions are not so easily categorized.

Under the Red Window section of the Table of Contents, eleven feelings are given with one or more creative suggestions for each. These feelings may be experienced at any age of our lives because feelings are more closely tied to circumstances and experiences than to age levels. All of the ideas suggested to explore these feelings in this section are geared to elementary age children because all of these activities have actually been used with this age level. But they can be used with other ages with minor changes. Here's where your creativity comes in.

In the Indigo Window section, the statements given indicate the value of this kind of thinking. One or more ideas beneath each negative fact illustrate this perspective. Many young adults are coming back into our churches. Other young adults who have grown up in the church are seeking directions of ministry for our day. Both of these situations give rise to doubts and questions—Indigo Window approaches. For this reason the participation experiences in this section are written mainly for young adults and have been tried out with that age group. With some changes and variations they can be used with older elementary and youth classes as well as seasoned adults. Again—be creative!

All ages can catch a Yellow Window glimpse of God. This section speaks to a variety of ages in the Sunday school. Some ideas are for individual enlightenment, some for group envisioning. Since dreams and visions cannot be pinned down, "approaches" are suggested and ideas suggested for each approach.

For clarification and an easy way to locate specific activities for each age, the Age-Level Index is included on pages 87-88.

•FACTS•
LOOKING OUT THE WHITE WINDOW

The time is surely coming, says the Lord God,
*   when I will send a famine on the land;*
not a famine of bread, or a thirst for water,
*   but of hearing the words of the Lord.*
                                    —Amos 8:11

"You shall love the Lord your God with all your heart, and with
all your soul, and with all your mind." This is the greatest and
first commandment.
                                    —Matthew 22:37-38

Dictionary definition
MIND: intellect

INTRODUCTION TO WHITE WINDOW TEACHING

White window teaching is bright, clear, and intense; the focus is narrow. Looking out the white window (teaching neutral facts) is probably the easiest way to teach Sunday school because it is most like public school teaching with which we are most familiar, and because we often feel more secure in what it is we are supposed to be doing. White window teaching can also be evaluated. We can know if we have met our goal. If, for example, we are attempting to teach the Ten Commandments as a list to be learned, it is fairly easy to find out if the students have learned the list.

How important is white window teaching in the Sunday school? We have all encountered persons who know all about God but do not know God, and persons who know the information in the Bible but not the God of the Bible. For this reason I would not put it as our most important task. But there are certain basic skills and bodies of information that we need to know. More and more we are getting requests for remedial Bible study. As the passage from Amos prophesies, there is a thirst for hearing the Word of God. The point of white window teaching is to build skills and background information that will serve as a foundation to our further nurturing of faith.

Now that we know what it is we are attempting to do, how can we bring our creativity into play? What are some creative approaches to white window teaching?

Practice getting into this mode of teaching by doing this exercise:
List three things from your upcoming Sunday school lessons that you feel completely neutral about.

1.

2.

3.

Where, in your lesson material, do you find that which needs to be taught as neutral information? Mark this in your lesson with a white window.

A nonverbal way to prepare yourself for teaching in this manner is to get with another teacher and play the game Mirror Image.

Stand facing your partner. You are the mirror. You have to follow all of your partner's movements exactly. If he moves his hand, you move your hand in exactly the same way. If he smiles, you smile. Practice this for a few minutes. Follow the movements exactly! Now reverse and let the other partner be the mirror.

Just as in the game, white window teaching deals with only the facts. Never mind the interpretation. We just want neutral, objective facts.

Now, how shall we teach this neutral, nonemotional learning and reporting of facts which constitutes the white window category? There are ways of asking for information that leave out feelings, impressions, and opinions. Must white window teaching always be hard work and boring repetition? I think not. It can be playful, inventive, and creative. Journey with me through the Sunday school and let's explore white window learning at various age levels.

IN THE NURSERY (TODDLERS)

Our youngest children can begin to experience white window glimpses of God. As soon as they begin to notice things and say words, we can teach facts.

Fact: The Bible is our church's book.

IDEA #1 Teach the children to spell the word "Bible." Clap your hands at each letter. Let children take turns clapping and spelling alone for the rest of the class.

IDEA #2 Sing, to the tune of "The Farmer in the Dell":

The B-I-B-L-E. The B-I-B-L-E,
Hi ho the derry-o
The B-I-B-L-E.

IDEA #3 Play "Find the Bible." Put several books on your table. Ask the children to find the Bible. Walk with your children through other Sunday school classrooms. Can they find a Bible? Locate the Bible in your sanctuary.

IDEA #4 Let the very young children help you create a worship table. Place an open Bible on it. Say "This is our Bible." Take the children to gather flowers to place around the Bible.

Fact: The Bible has stories about Jesus.

IDEA #5 Show pictures of Jesus to the children. Use your curriculum material and other resources. Hang pictures of Jesus in your classroom. Ask often, "Who is this?" "Where do we find stories about Jesus?"

IDEA #6 Hold the Bible in your lap when you are telling Bible stories to the children.

IDEA #7 Teach the song "Jesus Loves Me."

IN THE PRE-SCHOOL

Fact: We can say words from the Bible.

IDEA #8 Learn the Golden Rule: "Do unto others as you would have them do unto you." Encourage this factual learning by giving stars and stickers. Let children take turns saying the verse aloud. Give the prizes to all the children each time one child says it correctly. As in *Alice in Wonderland* everyone gets prizes. Instead of competition, help the class feel proud when any of their members learns it. Cheer and shout "Hurrah."

Facts/
Looking
Out the
White Window

Fact: Families have Bibles at home.

IDEA #9 Create a Bible display. Send a letter to parents asking them to send a Bible from home with their child the next Sunday. Work with your class in arranging all the Bibles on a display table. Talk about the different Bibles. Let each child show and share his or her Bible. Have on hand some extra Bibles for those who for some reason have none.

Write the child's name on a card to place by the Bible. Invite the parents or other church members to see your display.

Fact: The pastor reads from the Bible.

IDEA #10 Take your class into the church sanctuary. Show them the large pulpit Bible if you have one. Ask your pastor to meet your class and tell them how he or she uses the Bible.

Fact: We can name people in the Bible.

IDEA #11 Tell stories from the Bible to your class. Follow with a musical game. The teacher stands in the center of a circle singing to the tune of "London Bridge":

"Who saw Jesus from a tree? from a tree? from a tree?
Who saw Jesus from a tree? Tell me now."
(Children answer "Zaccheus!")

"Who killed a giant with a sling? with a sling? with a sling?
Who killed a giant with a sling? Tell me now."
(Children shout "David!")

Create more verses to go with your stories.

Fact: We can say a creed.

IDEA #12 Echo reading.

Teacher: Say after me, just as I say it.
The teacher points to self and says:

I believe in God.
(Children echo.)
I believe in Jesus.

(Children echo.)
I believe God loves me.
(Children echo.)
The teacher points to the students:

You believe in God.
(Children echo.)
You believe in Jesus.
(Children echo.)
You believe God loves you.
(Children echo.)
The teacher points around the circle.

We believe in God.
(Children echo.)
We believe in Jesus.
(Children echo.)
We believe God loves us.
(Children echo.)

EARLY ELEMENTARY

Fact: The Old Testament is different from the New Testament.

IDEA #13 Play a game. Write "Old Testament" at one end of the room. Write "New Testament" at the other. The children stand in the middle. The teacher names a Bible character or story, then asks: "Where do we find the story? Old Testament or New Testament?" The children choose one side of the room as the correct side to stand in and move to that side.

1. (This part of the Bible tells about) time before the life of Christ. (OT)
2. Jesus is born. (NT)
3. God creates the world. (OT)
4. Abraham and Sarah follow God. (OT)
5. Jesus chooses special disciples. (NT)
6. Moses leads the people out of Egypt. (OT)
7. Jesus is killed. (NT)
8. Paul goes as a missionary. (NT)
9. Joseph forgives his brothers. (OT)
10. The Christian church begins. (NT)

Fact: Jesus had helpers.

IDEA #14 Learn the song "Twelve Disciples" to the tune of "Bringing in the Sheaves."

There were twelve disciples
Jesus called to help him:
Simon Peter, Andrew, James,
his brother John.
Philip, Thomas, Matthew,
James the son of Alpheus,
Thaddeus, Simon, Judas,
and Bartholomew.

Write the names of the twelve disciples on twelve pieces of construction paper and place one around each child's neck. If you have more than twelve in your class repeat the names. As the name is mentioned in the song, the child with the corresponding name jumps up, then sits down. Try removing the signs, four at a time, until the class is able to name all twelve disciples without signs.

Fact: We can learn the Lord's Prayer.

IDEA #15 Write the Lord's Prayer on a large blackboard. Say it over slowly with the children, asking them to pay close attention because you are going to erase five words afterward.

Our Father which art in heaven,
Hallowed be thy name.
Thy kingdom come. Thy will be done
in earth, as it is in heaven.
Give us this day our daily bread.
And forgive us our debts, as we forgive our debtors.
And lead us not into temptation,
but deliver us from evil:
For thine is the kingdom,
and the power,
and the glory, for ever.
Amen. (Matt. 6:9-13 KJV)

Erase these words: heaven (in line 1), earth, bread, temptation, and power.

Say the prayer with the children again, letting them fill in the words and telling them to look closely because you will be erasing more words next time. Then erase: Father, kingdom (in line 3), heaven (in line 4), debts, and evil.

Again, say the prayer with the class, letting them fill in the blanks and telling them to look at the remaining words carefully. This time erase: name, will, day, debtors, glory.

Congratulate those who are able to fill in all the blanks.

Fact: We can learn many things about Bible characters.

IDEA #16 After reading and studying about a Bible character such as David, review your facts with a rhythm. Divide the class into two teams. Each team talks together about all the facts about David the members know. After a few minutes the whole group comes together. The teacher and class slap both hands on their thighs in rhythm to four counts. When the rhythm is going well the teacher says:

David is known for many things.

The rhythm keeps going. First one team, then the other, thinks of something about David. They say it aloud in rhythm.

"He played on a harp."
or
"He tended the sheep."
or
"He became a great king."

Neither team can repeat what the other team has said. The game continues until the teams can think of no more facts. For young elementary children, this works best if there is an adult with each team.

IDEA #17 Play "Who am I?" List on the board all the Bible characters you have been studying. For example, if you have been studying the Old Testament you might list:

Abraham	Jacob	David
Sarah	Esau	Ruth
Isaac	Joseph	Moses

The teacher chooses a character and gives one fact about this character. For example, "I had a twin brother." The class may ask four questions. If the one answering gets it right on the first try he or she gets four points for the class. The teacher gives another fact. The class gets three points for getting it correct on this clue. The game continues with two points for the third clue and one point if the class gets it on the last clue. How big a score can the class get?

MIDDLE ELEMENTARY

Fact: We can learn about Bible lands and times.

IDEA #18 Play the game "Work in Bible Times." Write the words below on slips of paper. Give one to each member of your class. Half the class are workers. The other half are work. When the teacher says "Go," the children run and find their partner.

WORKERS	WORK
Jesus	carpenter
Paul	tentmaker
Peter	fisherman

| Shepherds | tend sheep |
| Farmers | plant seeds |

Fact: We can learn about people in the Bible.

IDEA #19 A true or false contest about Ruth.

All students stand. The teacher asks a question. A student answers "true" or "false." If the child misses, he or she sits down. If the answer is correct the child remains standing.

1. The story of Ruth begins in the country of Moab. (T)
2. Naomi was Ruth's mother. (F)
3. Naomi had two daughters-in-law. (T)
4. Opry Winfred was one daughter-in-law's name. (F)
5. Both daughters-in-law stayed with Naomi. (F)
6. Orpah left and went to New York. (F)
7. Naomi and Ruth caught a bus to Naomi's old home in Bethlehem in Judah. (F)
8. Boaz was Naomi's former husband. (F)
9. Boaz owned a field and was very wealthy. (T)
10. Ruth and Naomi had no money or food. (T)
11. Ruth's husband died after they had been married about ten years. (T)
12. When Ruth and Naomi arrived in Judah it was seed planting time. (F)
13. Naomi's husband was named Elimelech. (T)
14. Ruth's home country was Moab. (T)
15. Boaz was a kinsman of Ruth's husband. (T)
16. "Gleaning" means to gather what is left after the reapers have threshed a field. (T)
17. Wealthy people left some of their grain for the poor. (T)
18. Boaz thought Ruth was a fine young woman to leave her home country and take care of her mother-in-law. (T)
19. Boaz married Orpah. (F)
20. Ruth was an ancestor of Jesus. (T)

IDEA #20 Multiple choice about Moses.

Pick one of the three answers.
1. When Moses was born, his mother hid him for three months because
   a. this was the Jewish custom.
   b. Pharaoh was killing all baby boys.
   c. he was very ugly.

Answer: b

2. When she could hide him no longer she
   a. gave him to Pharaoh.
   b. left the village by night.
   c. placed him in a basket at the river's edge.

Answer: c

3. Moses was found by
    a. the Pharaoh's wife.
    b. the Pharaoh's daughter.
    c. his sister Miriam.

Answer: b

4. After the baby Moses was found
    a. his mother never saw him again.
    b. his mother became his nurse.
    c. the baby was sent back to his home.

Answer: b

5. The Pharaoh's daughter named the baby "Moses" because
    a. that was her favorite uncle's name.
    b. it meant "beloved."
    c. it meant "drawn out."

Answer: c

6. When Moses was grown and living in Midian he saw a strange sight one day. It was
    a. a burning bush that was not consumed.
    b. a burning house in the middle of the desert.
    c. a forest fire.

Answer: a

7. God spoke to Moses out of the burning bush and told him to
    a. go to Jerusalem.
    b. go to Memphis.
    c. go to the Pharaoh.

Answer: c

8. Moses
    a. was eager to lead his people.
    b. begged God not to send him.
    c. suggested God send his wife, Zipporah.

Answer: b

9. When Pharaoh refused to let the people of Israel go, how many plagues did God send?
    a. 3
    b. 10
    c. 12

Answer: b

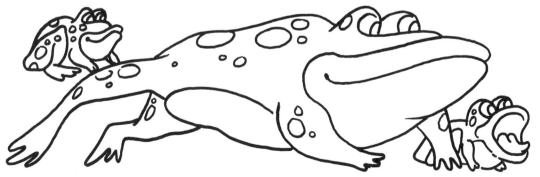

Facts/
Looking
Out the
White Window

10. When Pharaoh finally agreed to let the Israelites go
    a. he changed his mind and sent troops after them.

33

    b. he was relieved finally to be free of them.
    c. he sent guards to escort them into Canaan.

Answer: a

11. When the Israelites reached the Red Sea
    a. they swam across.
    b. they crossed on boats and rafts.
    c. the waters parted and they walked across.

Answer: c

12. While wandering in the desert the Israelites became hungry, so
    a. they stopped and cooked food they had brought with them.
    b. they ate food God supplied.
    c. they found a McDonald's.

Answer: b

13. When the Amalekites attacked the Israelites Moses went up on a mountain. The Israelites won the battle as long as
    a. Moses shouted instructions.
    b. the sun was on their left.
    c. Moses held his hands in the air.

Answer: c

14. Moses received the Ten Commandments from God
    a. hidden in a cave.
    b. when he went upon a mountain.
    c. in the sacred tent.

Answer: b

15. The people of Israel kept the Ten Commandments
    a. in a special temple they built.
    b. in an ark of gold that God designed.
    c. on parchment scrolls.

Answer: b

Fact: We can find the Bible book, chapter, and verse.

IDEA #21 Have a race. Each student will need his or her own Bible. The teacher calls out a well-known chapter and verse in the Bible, and the children try to see who can find it first.

1. Psalm 23 (shepherd's psalm)
2. John 3:16 (love verse)
3. I Corinthians 13 (Paul's chapter on love)
4. Galatians 5:22-23 (fruits of the Spirit)
5. Matthew 5:3-12 (the Beatitudes)
6. Matthew 19:13-15 (blessing of the children)
7. Acts 2:10 (coming of the Holy Spirit)
8. Mark 16:15 (sending forth)
9. Acts 9:1-19 (conversion of Saul)
10. Exodus 20:1-17 (Ten Commandments)

The white window methods suggested for older elementary grades can be adapted for youth and even adults by using harder questions. They can be adapted for younger children by using easier questions.

Fact: We can learn *who*.

A Who fact gives you the name of a person.

IDEA #22 Here are some important persons in the Bible described in a single sentence. Who was the person?

1. He denied Jesus three times in one night. (Peter)
2. He wrestled all night with a heavenly being. (Jacob)
3. He baptized Jesus. (John the Baptist)
4. She laughed when told she would have a baby. (Sarah)
5. She was chosen as a wife while drawing water for camels at the well. (Rebekah)
6. He was sold into slavery by his brothers. (Joseph)

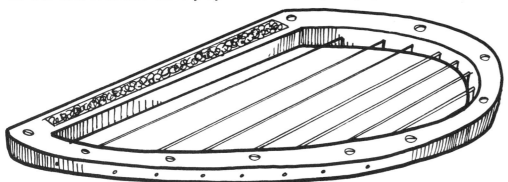

7. He played his harp before the possessed king and eased the king's spirit. (David)
8. He was the ruler at the time of Jesus' birth. (Herod)
9. He had a vision where he saw a valley of bones come to life. (Ezekiel)
10. He won a battle with trumpets, empty pitchers, and a lamp within the pitcher. (Gideon)
11. He replaced Moses as leader of the Israelites after Moses died. (Joshua)
12. He was a tax collector before becoming a disciple. (Matthew)
13. She was a great warrior/judge. (Deborah)
14. She was the first to see the resurrected Jesus. (Mary Magdalene)

Fact: We can learn *where*.

Where questions usually ask for facts about places.

IDEA #23 Play "String-Across." On a large bulletin board, mount the following names of biblical persons on the left side. On the right, mount names of places associated with these persons. Rearrange the places below so that they do not correspond to the name directly at left. Attach yarn beside the names and let students string the yarn to the correct place.

Jesus	Nazareth
Abraham	Ur
Joseph	Egypt
Moses	Sinai
David	Jerusalem
Joshua	Canaan
Isaiah	Babylon
Wise Men	Persia
Mary and Martha	Bethany
Adam and Eve	Garden of Eden

IDEA #24 To make the game more difficult, try this: where the disciples are supposed to have preached. Use the same string-across method.

Peter	Rome
Andrew	Greece
James the greater	Judea
John	Asia Minor
James the lesser	Palestine and Egypt
Jude	Assyria and Persia
Philip	Phrygia, Caesarea
Bartholomew	Armenia
Matthew	Africa
Thomas	Syria and India
Simon	Persia

Fact: We can learn *what*.

When we ask the question "What is happening today?" we go to the newspaper for answers. Newspaper articles carry headlines, which are short titles that answer the "what" question quickly.

IDEA #25 Write headlines. Give the members of your class Bible stories to read and have them write the headline that would accompany the story if it were to be in today's newspaper. From the last week of Jesus' life:

1. Palm Sunday narrative	Matthew 21:1-11
2. Cleansing the Temple	Matthew 21:12, 13
3. Last Supper	Matthew 26:20-30
4. The arrest	Matthew 26:47-56
5. The trial	Matthew 26:57-68
6. The Crucifixion	Matthew 27:32-54
7. The Resurrection	Matthew 28:1-10

Remind the students that in writing headlines you give facts only—not opinions.

Fact: We can learn *when*.

IDEA #26 Play the game "Which Came First?"

Divide the class into two teams. The teacher asks the question. The team may confer before answering. Each correct answer scores one point. Questions alternate from one team to the other.

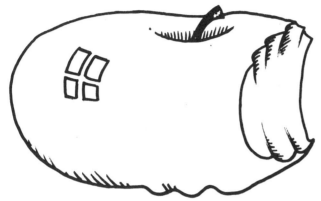

1. Did Eve bite the apple first or did Adam? (Eve)
2. Who was older, Cain or Abel? (Cain)
3. Which came first, the Tower of Babel or the Great Flood? (the Flood)
4. Which twin was born first, Jacob or Esau? (Esau)
5. Which plague came first, the lice or the frogs? (the plague of the frogs)
6. The commandment to love God or the commandment to love your neighbor as yourself? (to love God)
7. Which book in the Bible comes first, Leviticus or Exodus? (Exodus)
8. Psalms or Proverbs? (Psalms)
9. Matthew or Mark? (Matthew)
10. Thessalonians or Colossians? (Colossians)
11. Which person lived first, Moses or David? (Moses)
12. Jesus or Paul? (Jesus)
13. The beginning of the Christian church or the death of Jesus? (death of Jesus)
14. Deborah or Miriam? (Miriam)
15. Jesus chooses his disciples first or Jesus is tempted in the wilderness first? (tempted)
16. Joseph or Jacob lived first? (Jacob)
17. Solomon or David? (David)
18. Who visited Jesus first, the wise men or the shepherds? (the shepherds)
19. Which comes first, Palm Sunday or Good Friday? (Palm Sunday)
20. Which took place first, the Crucifixion or the Resurrection? (the Crucifixion)

Fact: We can learn *how long*.

"How long" questions ask for facts about numbers.

IDEA #27 The number 40 applies to each of these biblical situations. But 40 what? How long?

1. During the time of Noah it rained 40 _____ and 40 _____. (days and nights)
2. Moses and the children of Israel wandered in the desert for 40 _____. (years)
3. Moses fasted on Mount Sinai for 40 _____ and 40 _____. (days and nights)
4. The scouts searched the land of Canaan for 40 _____. (days)
5. Jesus fasted 40 _____ in the wilderness. (days)
6. Elijah fasted 40 _____ and 40 _____. (days and nights)
7. Jonah preached in Nineveh that the city would be destroyed in 40 _____. (days)
8. David was king of Israel for 40 _____. (years)
9. Solomon was king for 40 _____. (years)
10. After the Resurrection, Jesus appeared to the disciples for 40 _____ before the Ascension. (days)

Fact: We can learn hidden facts.

The first Christians often had to hide from the Roman soldiers and hold their meetings in secret.

IDEA #28 Break this early Christian code to discover the secret message. Then write a coded message of your own.

Nathan
ran
camel
meeting
eat
chair
monkey
tonight
soon
sheep
in
to
on
door
kitten
catacombs
let's
Josie

> Hint—Each word in the secret message follows the name of an animal.

Fact: White window teaching expands knowledge of biblical facts.

IDEA #29 Be a reporter. Get that story. A newspaper reporter asks who, what, where, when, and why. He or she tries to get all the facts about an event. Instead of a current situation, you will be taking that approach with a Bible story.

Step 1: Read Acts 12:1-9 (or any Bible story).
Step 2: Decide where your newspaper would be published and give it a name, for example, the *Jerusalem Daily News*.
Step 3: Write the answers to the five reporter questions.

Who _____

What _____

Where _____

When _____

Why _____

Step 4: Compare the newsstories.

IDEA #30 Report a legal question. In this case it is a rule given by God to the ancient Israelites. Your law deals with punishment for crimes committed.

Step 1: Read Leviticus 24:19-20.
Step 2: Summarize the law as it is stated.
Step 3: Can you explain why this law may have been given?
Step 4: Are there updates on the law? Read Matthew 5:38-39.
Step 5: Answer the question, Does this later ruling cancel the first law?

The class share their answers.

IDEA #31 Compare Bible stories.

Jesus feeds the multitudes in

Matthew 14:13-21
Mark 6:30-44
Luke 9:10-17
John 6:1-14

Facts/
Looking
Out the
White Window

Where do the accounts agree? Where disagree? What are the facts?

IDEA #32 True or False Definitions.

All answers are either true or false. If "true," all students in the class hold up one finger. If "false," they hold up two fingers. All students respond simultaneously.

1. "Apostle" is a Greek word meaning "the oldest male in the family." (False—it means "one who is sent")
2. The common language spoken by Jesus was Aramaic. (True)
3. The Ark of the Covenant was the name of Noah's boat. (False—it was the sacred chest in which the Ten Commandments were kept)
4. Baal was the heathen god worshiped by the ancient Egyptians. (False—by the inhabitants of Canaan)
5. Balm was the gum of a bush that grew in Gilead and which was valued for its healing properties. (True)
6. "Beatitude" is a Latin word meaning happy. (True)
7. "Beth" is a Hebrew word meaning "house" and is used in compound proper names such as Beth-lehem. (True)
8. "Bible" is a Greek word meaning "holy." (False—it means books)
9. The Old Testament was written chiefly in Hebrew. The New Testament chiefly in Greek. (True)
10. "Caesar" was the family name of the emperors in Rome. (False—it was a title for the Roman emperors)
11. A centurion was an officer in the Roman army who commanded a group of 100 men. (True)
12. The Pillar of Cloud was where Jacob laid his head during his dream of angels descending and ascending. (False—it was one of God's signs to the children of Israel on their journey to the Promised Land)
13. Demons in Bible times were spirits considered responsible for the presence of disease, insanity, and evil in human beings. (True)
14. All of the New Testament letters were written by Paul. (False)
15. Gleaning in the Bible was a special privilege reserved for the poor that allowed them to gather grain or fruit after a field was harvested. (True)
16. Golgotha, where Jesus was crucified, was within the city of Jerusalem. (False—it was outside the city walls)
17. "Hosannah" is a Hebrew word meaning "palms." (False—it means "save now")
18. Manna was the food that Jesus used to feed the 5,000. (False—food supplied by God to the children of Israel on the journey to the Promised Land)
19. "Messiah" is a Hebrew word denoting anyone anointed with holy oil and set apart for high office. (True)
20. Maundy (Thursday) is from the Latin word for "to command." (True)

IDEA #33 Write a rap or a rhyme. Silly rhymes are good methods of learning the order of something. Create a silly rhyme or a rap for the seven days of Creation—two lines for each day.

To refresh your memory and for some rhyming words, read the following:

1. God created light (day) and darkness (night).
2. God separated heavens, sky, and earth.
3. God separated the seas and dry land and covered the earth with grass and trees.
4. God created sun, moon, stars.
5. God created fishes, birds.
6. God created animals—great and small, every creeping thing, and man and woman.
7. God was at rest.

Here is a rap created by the Christian Educators Fellowship of the Mississippi Conference of The United Methodist Church. First they wrote the words, setting them to a rap rhythm.

Chorus:

> *That was the week that was*
> *When God was on a roll*
> *He made a lot of things*
> *Out of a big dark hole.*
>
> *God was bored with all this dark*
> *So he created light*
> *Then he named the lighttime "day"*
> *And called the darktime "night."*
>
> *The second day he saw*
> *That he had made a pie*
> *Turned it on its side*
> *The earth beneath the sky.*
>
> *Then he kept the dry from wet*
> *And called it land and seas*
> *He covered it with green stuff*
> *And named it "grass" and "trees."*
>
> *The fourth day God was getting tired*
> *But found he wasn't done.*
> *He flung the stars and moon up high*
> *Then made a blazing sun.*

Facts/
Looking
Out the
White Window

God wanted to go fishing.
Cause seafood is delicious
And so he filled up all the seas
With big and little fishes.

God was there all by himself
And he was lonely still
He made all sorts of animals
And finally, Jack and Jill.

And on the seventh day God said
"It's time to take a rest
I'll rest from all the work I've done
I know I've done my best."

Here's another rap, from another group in the conference.

The Genesis story is really a snap
When you can say the creation rap

On the first day God made day and night
Looked all around, said "This is all right"

On day 2 she made the earth and sky
Put the earth down low and the sky up high.

Three days a comin, here comes the seas
Flowered up the land with grass and trees.

On day #4 she was having such fun
Made the moon and the stars and the sun.

Swimming and flying was what next occurred
So Day #5 brought fishes and birds.

Six days a running still looking bare
So God made animals to roam down there

Aardvarks, elephants, beetles and mice
God leaned back and said "This here's nice!"

Still something missing, What can it be?
There's nothing down there that's much like me.

Then to cap off her wondrous plan
God made woman and God made man.

On the 7th day God had finished the test
So she looked around and decided to rest.

And on that day God took a nap
And that, my friends, is the Creation Rap.

There is an additional interesting way to use white window teaching. This is particularly effective with adults.

Often our facts are embedded in arguments largely based on opinion. Listen carefully at your next group meeting and notice how often we come to meetings with our minds made up, using facts to bolster our arguments. We hammer our theories into shape with opinion, adding facts to harden them.

The white window offers a way to use facts as seeds to suggest ideas. Facts are just laid out on the table—neutral and objective. Just the facts— no opinions or comments. In this approach your own opinion is never permissible. This becomes a discipline that encourages the student to separate quite clearly in his or her own mind what is fact and what is interpretation.

Following are some situations we might face in our churches. These situations sometimes carry emotional overtones. For our purposes we will approach them using only facts.

1. Tell me why you are (or are not) teaching Sunday school, using only *facts*.
2. Tell me why you use curriculum from a certain denomination (you decide which). Give your white window reasons.
3. Why should (or should not) a woman minister be assigned to your church? Only *facts*. No opinions.

There are situations in our churches that have emotional overtones. Sometimes it is best to approach these from the white window. Remember, white indicates neutrality. Whenever you question people about ideas on which they have strong opinions they tend to sprinkle in facts that show their point of view in a favorable light. White window viewing helps us here by forcing us to avoid opinion and give *just* the facts.

•FEELINGS•
LOOKING OUT THE RED WINDOW

Search me, O God, and know my heart.
—Psalm 139:23a

"You shall love the Lord your God with all your heart, and with all your soul, and with all your mind." This is the greatest and first commandment.

—Matthew 22:37-38

Dictionary definition
HEART: source of the emotions

INTRODUCTION TO RED WINDOW TEACHING

Moving from the white window we now approach the red window, the window of feelings. The red window is nearly the opposite of the white window.

Looking out the red window we seek to open ourselves to our feelings and emotions and nonrational thinking, and through these get our glimpse of God. In making the important connection between what we have learned and what we are living, feelings create the bridge.

This kind of teaching gives us a chance to say "Well, that's how I feel about the matter!" It legitimates the emotions and feelings as an important part of learning. We open our hearts to God as well as our minds.

In using this type of teaching, we must always keep in mind that we do not need to make any attempt to justify our feelings or to provide a logical basis for them. Isolating our styles of learning, identifying red window learning, is affirmation enough.

In our technological society we place value on the measurable, the visible. Feelings embarrass us. Children are instructed "Don't cry," "Don't let them see how you feel," and we build walls that stifle us and crush creativity, which often finds its source in feelings.

The Sunday school classroom is one place where feelings can be accepted. By designating "red window" we are saying "It's O.K." We do not ever need to apologize for our feelings. They are what make us human. We do not need to treat them as extensions of logic. They come from a different source.

The most helpful attitude is to allow feelings fully into consciousness, to be aware, to notice, without assuming we have to act or explain or justify. In red window teaching we not only allow, we, as teachers, do all we can to provide the climate.

There are two kinds of feelings:

1. Ordinary emotions as we know them:

"I feel disappointed that my class was excluded from the Christmas pageant."

"I feel angry that no parents would volunteer to go on the overnight with the youth."

"I feel excited about the attendance at the senior citizens' program."

"I felt very moved by the Good Friday service."

Give a chance in meetings and the classroom for feelings to surface. They are there. If emotions and feelings are not permitted as input they lurk in the background and affect learning in a hidden way. We react. We feel.

In our classroom we can ask: "Looking out the red window, how are you feeling right now about this?" Resentment and sulking are brought out in the open. The red window provides a definite channel for feelings and emotions. We need no longer try to guess feelings. This is a means of asking for them directly.

In teaching situations, children often express feelings nonverbally—sulking, moping, fighting. Helping children express feelings in words not only helps them feel loved and understood but also prevents many unnecessary conflicts. It also helps disturbing feelings disappear. Let people express all feelings, including negative ones. No one wants to listen to rational explanations until they are convinced that the other person understands and accepts how they feel.

2. The other kind of feelings are hunch and intuition, impressions, imaginative insight. We react and feel rather than proceed from one rational step to the next. We will touch more on these at the yellow window.

I heard a woman say, "In my family if something wasn't rational, it didn't exist. At the same time I had intuitive sensings and even direct experiences that were not rational. I soon learned not to share these experiences. When I did I was labeled as weak and stupid."

If this has ever been your experience stop reading now and affirm yourself. We are wonderfully made, and being in touch with your feelings may be your creative gift.

In addition to allowing your students to acknowledge and express their feelings, you can create an environment in your classroom that surrounds that student with love and understanding. There seems to be a desperate hunger for this in our society today. Listen to your hunches. The "truth" may be found in how you feel.

What tools shall we use for this kind of learning? What do we take with us to the red window?

The arts open up feelings. The senses get us in touch with our feelings. Colors, textures, and movement open up feelings. Empathy for another is based on feelings.

The ways we learn from these sources are quite different from the ways we learn from logic. Red window learning is very personal, yet all persons experience some of the same feelings. Thus, feelings can be a wonderful bridge between persons. When a person touches your feelings you begin to think he or she is special. Jesus had the gift of touching persons' feelings.

You can learn to identify this type of teaching in your curriculum. When you run across it say, "This is red window learning. We are dealing now with our feelings." Perhaps you would like to stop reading now and identify red window teaching in your upcoming Sunday school lesson. Mark such sections with a red window.

Remember the rule: Everyone's feelings are accepted.

Let's get in touch with them.

In this chapter we will look at some common feelings: boredom, anger, jealousy, greed, loneliness, joy, grief, love. In addition we will look at situations that result from strong feelings: betrayal, prejudice. Ways are suggested to bring forth these feelings in your church school classrooms, to identify and affirm them, and to find similar experiences in the lives of Bible persons. By using this approach in your Sunday school class, the relevancy of faith becomes apparent.

We avoid boredom when we are using the red window approach because students are interested and motivated when their feelings are touched.

RED WINDOW FEELINGS

Feeling: Boredom

Boredom comes in both small and large doses to everybody, and there may be some of it every day. Here are some ideas for handling it.

IDEA #34 Writing and pondering.

Great joy and contentment come when we examine the minutest particulars of our daily living. Everyday things can grow mute with familiarity, so known they become unknown. The hymn, "Open My Eyes" says "that I may see glimpses of truth." Perhaps persons who find themselves bored with their lives could come to enjoyment by becoming sensitive to glimpses of truth.

Nature is an obvious source for these glimpses. Take your class outside for a glimpsing experience. Instruct them to move apart from one another and look intensely at things around them. To listen, notice the touch and maybe even taste of things. And then to write a phrase of not more than ten words that will articulate and make possible the sharing of this experience and perceptions. Instruct the students to concentrate on capturing *this* experience, this sudden intimate seeing that they wish to remember. They should feel free to let an object or event touch them.

This writing teaches the students not only to respect the experience of others but also to recall and treasure their own experiences. We become aware of the intimate things that touch us. We learn to trust the present, this moment, this actual seeing.

Give the class these criteria for their writing:

1. Is it brief?
2. Does it present a vivid image?
3. Does the image create an emotion without telling what emotion it is?

Boredom has a selfish side. It often comes when we do not relate to anything beyond ourselves. Glimpses force us outward to a consideration of the unity of nature. They help us be aware of life while we are living it.

Invite students to share their "glimpses." By sharing with others we let them into our lives in a very special, personal way.

IDEA #35 Tell your class this Moses story.

One day Moses was out in the fields. He was looking at the beauties and wonders of nature when he saw a flame of fire burst forth from a bush on the mountainside. He watched, expecting to see the bush destroyed by the fire, but the flame kept burning and no harm came to the bush.

"What a strange sight. I must take a closer look at this unusual bush, which flame cannot harm."

As he started forward he heard a voice speak to him from the flame. "Moses—Do not come near this bush. Put off the shoes from your feet, for you are standing on holy ground."

Moses understood, for people in those lands always removed their shoes when they approached a sacred place. So he stooped down quickly to loosen and remove his sandals. The voice said, "I am God and I have heard the cries and sorrows of my people. I am going to bring them out of Egypt to a promised land."

Moses had to turn aside to see. What would have happened if he had just kept on going? God is still very close to us, but we have to be looking and waiting. Maybe we passed a burning bush today but didn't turn aside to see or even notice it.

Ponder: Think of the most puzzling, ambiguous, bewildering thing you have *ever* seen. Try to imagine various explanations. Think about this: There is no such thing as ordinary experience but only a series of unusual events that people melt down to the ordinary because of lack of attention and creativity.

Feeling: Anger

We all know what anger is. This idea seeks to help us understand its feeling stages.

IDEA #36 Boiling water—the story of Saul.

(CAUTION is required in using this idea.)

Take your class to a kitchen. Put a pan of water on the stove to boil. Instruct your class to watch in silence. Ask them to compare what they are watching to experiences of anger in their lives.

The water is still at first, then it begins to simmer. The boiling starts slowly. Then as the intensity grows it begins to hiss. If allowed to continue the boiling becomes furious and the scalding water bursts out of the pan.

Move the class to a safe distance but point out how the water can scald anyone within range.

Ask the class to reflect on these questions: Why do people lose their temper? Do you remember a time when you lost your temper? Why did you lose it? Did your anger follow the steps of the boiling water?

The Bible affirms over and over the powerful grip of anger. Read about Saul's anger (I Sam. 18:6-10). Compare Saul's anger with the boiling water.

I Samuel 18:6-10—the simmering begins.
I Samuel 19:8-12—the boiling erupts; hissing begins.
I Samuel 20:30-34—The boiling becomes furious. The scalding anger spills out on Jonathan.

Remember and share a time when it appeared that violence might or did erupt around you.

Recall a time when you were part of a crowd that became disruptive and you were swept up in the unruly anger.

Consider this question: Does God get angry? Read Isaiah 2:6-22. Verse 19 says that people will hide in caves in the rocky hills or dig holes in the ground to try to escape the Lord's anger and to hide from his power and glory.

If possible, cautiously pour the boiling water outdoors on the earth. Watch it seep in and spread out. Compare this with the Bible verse above.

Ponder: What would make God angry? What is an appropriate focus of God's rage?

Feeling: Jealousy

Jealousy arises when we want something that someone else has and we have not. It may be physical, mental, emotional, economic, social, or financial. The exaggeration of these desires to the point of intensity creates jealousy.

IDEA #37 In the ancient Japanese Kabuki theater, when an actor applied makeup, he was said to draw lines of color on his face that traced the pattern or route the blood takes as it flows through the veins. Try this experience with your class:

Step 1: Provide washable Magic Markers in a variety of colors.
Step 2: Read the story of Joseph and his brothers (Gen. 37:1-11).
Step 3: Identify the feelings—jealousy producing hate and anger.
Step 4: Make faces illustrating these emotions.
Step 5: With Magic Markers, accent the lines the emotions etch on the faces. Consider appropriate colors. You have heard the expression "green with envy." Why green? Do you associate red with anger? What colors seem most expressive to you?
Step 6: The class share their faces.
Step 7: Wash up.

Ponder: Remember a time when you felt jealousy. How intense was the feeling? Did you act on these feelings? Jealousy is a common feeling. Accept this feeling in yourself without judgment or need for justification. Recall the story of Joseph's brothers. The people in the Bible felt the same feelings we feel.

Feeling: Greed

Greed is an encroaching feeling that can splash over into other degenerating feelings (insensitivity to those around us, excessive dependence on luxuries and ease, pride and haughtiness).

Our society today encourages young people to build their lives around money and getting money. Youth are often encouraged to go for jobs that pay well without consideration of talents and service to others. Your feeling about money tells a lot about you personally. Consider Isaiah 55:2: "Why do you spend your money for that which is not bread,/and your labor for that which does not satisfy?"

IDEA #38 Storytelling drama—the story of Lazarus.

Storytelling is often the means by which the child first participates imaginatively in emotions and experiences of others. To illustrate this emotion, first gather the children around you in a setting that suggests that of ancient storytelling. They might sit on the floor around an imaginary campfire, or one corner of your room might be the storytelling corner. A tree in a large pot might be the storytelling tree under which you all gather.

When the children are settled, set a dramatic mood by beginning with the words often used by African storytellers: "A story is coming . . ."

Part 1

There was a certain rich man who thought only of his own comfort and happiness. He was not just rich, he was very rich. He didn't have just wealth, he had abounding wealth. He dressed in purple and fine linen. A robe of fine linen was worth five times its weight in gold. Even kings of great kingdoms did not dress finer. This man spent his days in luxury eating the finest food. Many servants jumped to do his bidding. His slightest wish was granted. He did nothing except to live and enjoy himself. He lived flamboyantly and ostentatiously every day.

There was also a poor man named Lazarus. He had no home or friends, but he was a good man who loved God. He lacked all the things just necessary for living. He sat at the ornate gate in front of the rich man's house begging for the bits of food that fell from the rich man's table. Unable to take care of his health, sores broke out on his body. The stray dogs who roamed the city came and licked at his sores. He was unable to drag himself away.

The rich man did not try to help him at all. He let him lie there day after day in his misery.

But this is not the end of the story. Something came to them both. What was it? The beggar died. The rich man also died. That's how it ends for all. Now, draw the veil and look beyond. Is there a difference? Yes.

Now the poor beggar was at rest in a place of peace and happiness. He was comforted. The rich man found himself in anguish, uttermost dejection, banished and sinking, resulting from his neglect of God.

The rich man cried out loudly for mercy. He asked that Lazarus come with just a drop of water to cool his burning tongue. But he was answered, "Remember that you enjoyed good things in your lifetime, while Lazarus had only poverty and suffering in the world. Now he is comforted and you are being tormented. Nothing can be sent to you because no one can pass from this place to your place of torment, nor can anyone from your place come to us."

Part 2

The teacher says, "Now we move to a deeper experience of this story. We have heard the facts. We have heard the parable as Jesus told it. Now let's expand upon it. Let's set the scene and identify with the characters. Let's try to get in touch with the feelings."

One child comes forward. Teacher says: "_____, you are the rich man." Teacher brings out velvet robes or capes, a silk scarf. "Feel all these fine textures" (put these robes on the child). "Now sit here." (Child is seated with feet elevated on a stool and lots of pillows all around.)

Four more children come forward. These are servants. One is given a brush to brush the rich man's hair. One is given lotion to put on his hands. One fans him with a fan. Another brings him chocolate candy and feeds him. (Real articles may be used or you may just pantomime the props.)

The teacher next chooses someone to be Lazarus. Put an old burlap bag around the child. This child sits on the floor.

Two other children are the dogs that come to lick Lazarus' sores. They snarl and growl and imitate the dogs.

Now all the children return to their seats except the rich man and Lazarus. The children choose partners and decide how they will come before the rich man and Lazarus, responding in a way they feel is appropriate. For example, they may come to the rich man and each child kiss a hand. They may come to Lazarus and sniff and walk away. Give each pair a few minutes to decide on their responses. Then each pair comes forward until all have had a chance to respond.

Teacher: In the second part of the parable, the roles are reversed. (The child playing Lazarus now comes and sits on the cushions, and the child playing the rich man crouches on the floor.) Each pair again responds to the characters, but this time they honor Lazarus and disdain the rich man.

By acting out parts and expressing feelings the story becomes more and more familiar to the students. The parable must become unforgettable for deeper levels of meaning to begin emerging.

Part 3

Now how can this story become my story? How does this parable connect with *my* life? Listen one more time to the story and then we'll play the game "Hold On—I Was There That Day."

The teacher reads the story, this time from the Bible (Luke 16:19-31).

Each child is instructed to remember a feeling or situation like a character in the story. Each child adds something to the story beginning with the words: "Hold on—I was there that day." For example, "Hold on—I was there that day because I have had a day when all I cared about was enjoying myself and having others wait on me. It was like this . . ."

Or,

"Hold on—I was there that day because once I was really, really hungry and no one would give me anything. It happened like this . . ."

Or,

"Hold on—I was there that day because I usually never think about or notice people in need, but one day I noticed . . ."

The ability of stories to carry on a life of their own, to seek out their own hearers, to tell us more than is told by us, opens up new possibilities for us in understanding deeper feelings.

This method—story, drama, personalizing—could be applied to all of the Bible stories used to illustrate feelings in this chapter.

Feeling: Loneliness

Loneliness is an intense inner feeling that something is missing. Sometimes there is almost an other-worldly homesickness. The feeling is captured in Psalm 107:4: Some wandered in the trackless desert and could not find their way to a city to live in. They were hungry and thirsty and had given up hope.

Try to get in touch with this feeling within yourself. It is a deep feeling that something is irretrievably lost—a time when we had direct access to God—a lost Eden. Loren Eisely, a writer and naturalist, describes it as messages that God has sent to humanity that somehow the messenger has gotten wrong. Implied in this is our feeling that life demands an answer from us, that an essential part of being human is the struggle to remember the meaning of the message. We are not what we seem. We have had a further instruction.

IDEA #39 Experiencing an old legend—the story of Pentecost.

The following experience seeks to capture the feeling of loneliness. It is designed for a sanctuary setting.

Before the service:
1. Put candles in each seat.
2. Arrange for ushers and go over their assignments with them.
3. Arrange for an organist or pianist to play the hymn "Spirit of God, Descend upon My Heart" (or similar hymn from your tradition).

A Pentecost Experience

Read Acts 2:1-13.
Leader: We know how to celebrate Christmas because Christmas is a wonderful story and we know how to tell a story. We know how to celebrate Easter because Easter is a victory and we know how to celebrate victories. But Pentecost is a happening—how do you celebrate a happening? We can retell the story, but it is such a strange story, a story of our heritage and one we no longer experience. We have never experienced tongues of fire or swirling winds.

Interesting enough, even Peter had trouble explaining to the people what was going on—were the disciples drunk?

A legend captures our experience. Once humans knew how to go into a sacred forest, light a sacred fire, say the sacred words—and the Spirit would come. As years passed humankind forgot the sacred words but still went into the sacred forest, lit the sacred fire, and the Spirit came.

More years passed. Humankind forgot how to make the sacred fire, but the priest still went into the sacred forest to the sacred place and the Spirit came.

Now, in our day, we have forgotten even the sacred place, and the Spirit does not come.

All we recognize, somewhere in our primordial memory, is that once we did this. We remember more than we know.

In the same haunting way we remember Pentecost. We have the story that once this happened, but we have forgotten the words that make us understood by all. We have forgotten how to make the fire that produces tongues of flame. We have forgotten the kind of place where Christians are together in prayer, and the Spirit does not come. The Power is still there, but we don't know how to tap it.

What then can we do? We can re-create in a small way and hope the happening occurs again.

Though the tongues of fire may not appear over our heads, we can hold a flame in our hands. Candles are in your seat. The ushers will light the candles on each aisle. Please pass your light down.

This is our tongue of fire. Contrived, but fire is the same—the flame is the same. Look at your candle. Watch the life in it that causes it to quiver. The flame is a delicate thing—a precious thing—the least little wind could put it out. This flame is like the Spirit of God in our heart. It is here. We kindle it and protect it until it grows and gives great warmth.

We have the fire. What of the sound of a strong wind blowing? We have only our small breaths, Lord, but it is the same wind. Hold your hand, the one not holding the candle, in front of your face. Feel your own breath. Like the tides of the ocean, our breath goes in and out. The rhythm of life is with us. Listen to the words of the hymn "Spirit of God, Descend upon My Heart." If you know the words, sing along. If not, be aware of your own breathing, in and out.

In the Pentecost story the disciples did not stay contemplating the fire and wind, but, as the story goes, they rushed out and began talking about the great things that God had done. Blow out your candle now. Turn to the person beside you and tell that person the last great thing God has done for you.

The coming of the Pentecost Spirit is a happening—a gift of God. But we know it did happen once, and if we can find the place, kindle the fire, remember the words, it can happen again.

Feeling: Grief

Grief is a devastating experience, touching us deeply.

IDEA #40 Use body movements. Read about the disciples' grief in Luke 23:26-49. Identify two kinds of grief.

1. personal grief
2. the grief of another

Remember a time when you were forced to stand by helpless while someone else suffered. To empathize and understand how another person is feeling, learn from your body. Use body movements to get in touch with feelings of grief.

Stand facing a partner. Play a charade in which players act out an emotion with only one body part. The teacher instructs the students which feeling to express and which body part to use.

Show with your eyes—pain
Show with your walk—sorrow
Show with your hands—loss
Show with your head—grief
Show with your arms—heartache
Show with your mouth—misery
Show with your posture—despair
Show with your shoulders—anguish

Empathy is the ability to feel the way another feels. It is putting yourself in someone else's shoes. If a friend is hit, you say "ouch"—that's empathy.

Try to understand through the body movements you have just used the great grief of those followers of Jesus watching the crucifixion.

Personal Grief

One-on-one, share your time of great grief. Talk about what helped. These suggestions have worked for others in times of great grief:

1. Treat yourself gently and positively.
2. Try writing your feelings out. This is sometimes easier than speaking.
3. Avoid exhaustion. Take hot baths, long walks, gentle exercise, and eat right. Pamper yourself.
4. Stay away from pessimistic people who are angry or morose.
5. Stay close to family and close friends.

Feeling: Joy

Intense joy has an element of surprise in it. It is a feeling of being overwhelmed by life in a new way.

IDEA #41 Experience joy through textures and sounds. Read Exodus 14:1-30. Ask the students to shut their eyes and in their imaginations try to capture the feelings that the Israelites must have been experiencing: mortal fear as they saw the approaching enemy, distrust of their leader, self-pity at having been led to this situation, desperation at what looked like a hopeless situation—then wide-eyed wonder, incredulous amazement, surprising, overwhelming joy.

Words cannot capture the experience and the feelings such an event engendered. It changed the course of history, and to this day, descendants are instructed to remember.

In later years, Isaiah wrote Isaiah 43:16-17: Long ago the Lord made a road through the sea, a path through the swirling waters. He led a mighty army to destruction, an army of chariots and horses. Down they fell never to rise, snuffed out like the flame of a lamp.

Have on hand a variety of small scraps of fabric—burlap, satin, net—in a variety of colors. Say these words slowly to the class, asking them to create mental pictures the words suggest:

overjoyed	gleeful	ecstasy
gladness	cheerful	happiness
delighted	blissful	rapturous
wonder	marvel	astonishment
amazed	dazzled	flabbergasted
awed	unexpected	miraculous
indescribable	unutterable	stupendous

Now instruct the students to open their eyes and pick colors and textures of material that most accurately reflect the texture of their feelings. Ask them to paste or staple the material on paper as a reminder and expression of their feelings. Invite the class to share.

Utterances and sounds are often our first response to surprising joy— brief snippets of language. *Roget's International Thesaurus* gives these expressions, among others, under "awe":

Feelings/
Looking
Out the
Red Window

really!	odzooks!	did you ever!
good heavens!	zounds!	you don't say!
my stars!	who would have thought it!	blow me down!

Ask your students if they have ever heard or used these expressions. What do they use?

"Hallel" is a nonverbal sound of great joy used in the Near Eastern world. It is a trilling sound. The word "Hallelujah" comes from it. Ask someone to illustrate a "hallel" to your class and then all try it together—an exciting experience!

Miriam's response to the great event of crossing the Red Sea was to sing, shake tambourines, and dance—an appropriate response. Intense joy can never be captured using just spoken language.

Feeling: Love

Love comes first to mind as the feeling we wish to engender in our church school classroom. Is there any teacher who does not sincerely want his or her students to feel enveloped in love—to experience some wave of the great ocean of God's love? In our classes we hope to generate the imperative to love. Sunday school should be one place children can always feel wanted and cared about, accepted for themselves, just the way they are.

IDEA #42 Rhythmic movement.

With the African folksong "Jesu, Jesu," children use music and movement to deepen and broaden their understanding of love. A star, the symbol for God's gift of love in Jesus, is the form taken by this dance. Have the class listen to the music first, feeling the strong rhythmic beat. Children stand in circles of five and number off 1 through 5.

Refrain:

"Jesu"

Children get ready.

"Jesu"

All children in circle raise right hands, palms out.

"fill us with your love"

Child 1 touches child 2's upraised palm with her palm on the word "us," then swings right arm back. On the word "love," child 1's arm starts swinging forward and up to touch the palm of child 3 (moving slightly out in the direction of child 3) on the word "us."

"show us how to serve"

Child 1 touches palm lightly with child 3's upraised palm and then swings right arm backward reaching backward arc on the word "serve."

"the neighbors we have"

Child 1 moves slightly toward child 4. The swinging rhythm of the arm of child 1 comes forward to touch the upraised palm of child 4 on the word "neighbors." On "have" the arm again completes the backward swing and swings forward.

"from you."

Child 1 moves slightly toward child 5 and touches child 5's upraised palm on the final word "you."

During the following verse, the children join hands and circle to the left singing:

Kneels at the feet of his friends
silently washes their feet

Then the children circle to the right singing:

Master who acts as a slave
to them.

On the second refrain, movements identical to those above are undertaken with child 2 taking the lead, touching the palms of the other children in the star formation, and stepping slightly toward each of the other children at the appropriate time.

The children continue to follow the same directions, circling on the verse and touching upraised palms on the refrain. Each of the five children gets an opportunity to be the leader in the refrain. Child 1 before verse 1, child 2 before verse 2, and so on.

As teachers we ponder: Am I embodying love in my classroom? What am I teaching today that will make my students more loving and more open to love?

Feeling: Happiness

What would you like to see happen to make you the happiest person in the world? Jot down privately what comes first to your mind.

Taking a little more time, ponder these ideas: There are many things in life that make us very happy. Think of one special one. What was the happiest thing that ever happened to you? Why did it make you happy?

Now consider these definitions of happiness: From the ancient Greeks: The key to happiness would be the exercise of one's talents for others. Martin Luther King, Jr.: You have to find something worth dying for. Read Jesus' words on happiness in Matthew 5:3-11.

All seem to say that happiness requires forgetting oneself. Do you agree?

IDEA #43 Choosing pictures.

Assemble a pile of pictures from your curriculum materials. For example, illustrations of Jesus and the lost sheep, Zaccheus, the boy with the loaves and fishes, modern family life pictures.

Let the children choose pictures that make them happy. Have on hand stickers of smiley faces. Instruct the children to paste the faces on the pictures that make them feel glad.

Discuss what they like about the pictures they chose.

IDEA #44 Sparklers—Mary's Song of Praise.

Read Mary's song of praise and happiness in Luke 1:46-55.

To experience this exuberant expression of happiness, stand in a wide circle. Give each student an unlit sparkler. Sing the hymn "My Soul Gives Glory to My God" or an appropriate hymn from your tradition. As the song is sung a leader with a lighted sparkler touches off the next one in the circle, and this continues around the circle until all are lit and extinguished.

This deep feeling of happiness is more profound than the buoyant feeling of joy.

Feeling: As a Member of a Minority

IDEA #45 A list poem—the story of Joseph sold into slavery.

Read Genesis 37:28. "When some Midianite traders passed by, they drew Joseph up, lifting him out of the pit, and sold him to the Ishmaelites for twenty pieces of silver. And they took Joseph to Egypt."

Step 1: Shut your eyes and imagine you are the only human in a room of cats; you are the only child in a room of adults; you are the only boy in a room of girls.

Step 2: With eyes still shut, try to imagine how Joseph felt all alone in the land of Egypt—the only Hebrew in a land of Egyptians. Think hard about how it would feel to be different in a crowd of people.

Step 3: The teacher writes this title on the board: "The Way Joseph Felt in Egypt." Accept answers from the class to the question above. Write all these answers on the board under the title. Do not comment. From time to time reread the lines starting with the title and continuing until you get approximately twenty answers.

Step 4: The class looks over the lines and chooses nine that best express feelings. Let the class choose the ones to keep. Explain to them again that they are to choose lines that evoke feelings.

Step 5: When the class has agreed on the nine lines, erase the others. This is your class poem on Joseph's feelings in Egypt.

Discuss: Is everyone part of a minority sometimes? What can we do to make outsiders feel a part of a group? Do we stereotype minority persons? What are some ways we do it?

Being in the minority takes many forms. Remember a time when you were uncomfortable being a Christian because no one else was, or, just a time when you've felt the most alone—forsaken—deserted.

Read this statement to the class: There may be more danger in prejudices that are founded in logic than in those acknowledged as emotions. Ask the class what they think this means. Is prejudice a feeling or a fact?

Feeling: Betrayal

Read Luke 22:54-62. Spend some time pondering this question: I wonder how Jesus felt when Peter betrayed him?

Bible stories may call up a story of our own. Remember a time when you felt betrayed by a friend. Let your mind move back and forth between Jesus' story and your own story.

Turn the story around and recall a time when you denied knowing someone or denied doing something because you feared the consequences. Were you discovered? What gave you away? How did you feel?

IDEA #46 Write your experience of betrayal but write it in the third person, as though it happened to someone else. Sometimes it is hard to tell someone else how you are feeling. It's too personal. So we share the event that makes us aware of these feelings. This helps the other person recall similar feelings of his or her own. Writing in the third person helps us deal with the event that produced the feeling. It gives us a little objective distance. Begin "Once upon a time there was . . ."

•NEGATIVE FACTS•
LOOKING OUT THE INDIGO WINDOW

I will give free utterance to my complaint.
I will speak in the bitterness of my soul.
I will say to God, Do not condemn me;
let me know why you contend against me.
                                                —*Job 10:1*

"You shall love the Lord your God with all your heart, and with all your soul, and with all your mind." This is the greatest and first commandment.

                                                —*Matthew 22:37-38*

Dictionary definition
MIND: *intellect*

INTRODUCTION TO INDIGO WINDOW TEACHING

A Charlie Brown cartoon says, "Just when I have a good idea—someone always brings up the budget!"

A recently appointed District Superintendent in The United Methodist Church, when asked how he liked his new job, replied, "I am learning to dread one day at a time."

Negative thinking. We move now to the indigo window. Is it possible to catch a glimpse of God through argument, criticism, and negative thinking? There are persons who come to faith through this perspective and their faith is powerful and strong. In fact, an unexamined, unquestioned faith seems smug and frigid. We must question continually—continually be open to new revelation. It may be more difficult to locate the indigo window in your curriculum. It may more nearly describe an attitude in your classroom.

Madeleine L'Engle in her book *Walking on Water* quotes an anonymous source: "God must be very great to have created a world which carries so many arguments against his existence."

In this section we will look at the ways indigo window gazing can be helpful.

First, a definition. The indigo window is negative judgment, why something will not work. The indigo window sees what is wrong, incorrect, and in error, or that doesn't fit with experience or accepted knowledge. The indigo window points out risks and dangers and faults in a design.

By compartmentalizing learning into window categories, we have a helpful way to deal with the student in our class who is negative by nature. Who among us has not had the experience of moving with a class to an exciting plan or goal only to have a negative voice deflate all our plans at the last minute?

Recently I had the experience of working on a teacher training event. The committee had progressed with enthusiasm to the point of agenda, staff, and date, when a staff person injected this statement: "Experience proves no one will turn out for this event."

What should we do now? Continue with plans or just give up? Obviously a new variable had been introduced. In our usual, scrambled type of planning, where we try to do everything at once, the tone will be mainly negative. By focusing directly on the negative, however, the indigo window actually limits negativity.

We need negative feedback. To hold back because we fear that the negative aspects will kill an idea is not what we seek. With the indigo window we can focus on objections and assimilate the negative into our planning. We can accept the negative fact of no one attending training events, not as an insurmountable argument but as an assessment of the past, with which we can deal.

After discussing the negative, we can say: "Let's move from the indigo window." This signals a clear and definite switch from the negative.

It is not unlike using the expression we often hear when someone wants to add a negative note: "I'm playing the devil's advocate." The negative is expressed and then we move on. Our task is not to view the negative as an obstacle but to look for the constructive criticism and to incorporate the criticism into our plan.

A successful entrepreneur said, "A complaint is a luscious, golden opportunity. The joy of a complaint, for me, is I have a live customer on the line."

INDIGO WINDOW FACTS

Fact: The negative gives us new perspectives.

There are times when a negative statement not only instructs us but also moves us to deeper understanding.

What negative facts need to be injected in the following situations? How might you give an indigo window response in these situations? How could you present a negative fact that would be helpful?

IDEA #47 Practice giving a helpful negative response.

1. Your teachers are planning on making a mosaic of beans and macaroni.
   Give an indigo window response.
   (Consider what using food as a craft item or plaything says to a hungry world.)
2. Your summer family life committee is planning a balloon release near the seashore.
   Give an indigo window response.
   (Consider the fact that whales and other sea creatures have died from ingesting balloons.)

3. On the church van there are seat belts only in the front seat. The youth are using the van for an extended trip.
Give an indigo window response.
(Consider the death rate in car accidents where seat belts are not used.)

Are there other situations you are now facing where an indigo window response needs to be injected?

IDEA #48 Look at Daniel's indigo window gazing. Write a news report.

Read Daniel, chapter 1. Daniel and his friends displayed a negative action in their refusal to eat the king's food. This refusal turned out to be a wiser course. Daniel had the courage to challenge what was considered a privilege by others. Daniel stood up and said "I think that is wrong."

Does Daniel's story call up any story for you? Was there a time when you or someone you know challenged something that others considered a privilege? What were the results?

Write this story as a news article. Stick with the facts and report the results. Share your articles.

Where in the church or society would God like for you to speak out with a courageous negative voice?

IDEA #49 Play the game "Hidden Errors." Study Moses' spies.

Being able to detect faults in a plan is a strength of indigo window gazing.

Use a game to set the scene. In this game, players try to find deliberate errors in their opponents' drawing.

Divide the class into two teams. Instruct each team to draw a picture with three deliberate errors. For example, pieces in the wrong places, missing parts. When the drawings are completed the teams exchange drawings. The object is to see which team can find all the errors first.

After playing the game, study Numbers, chapter 13. Look for these answers:
1. Why were spies chosen?
2. Who was sent?
3. What seven things were the spies to discover?
4. What were they to bring back? How did they carry it?
5. How long were they gone?
6. What did Caleb advise?
7. What did the other spies say?
Discuss the answers.

When the negative facts are before the Israelites what do they do next? Continue reading Numbers, 14:1-25. How did they use the negative information that was given them? Is this the usual way we handle negative facts? What were the ultimate results of their actions? Can you recall a situation where an action was needed, the prospects looked overwhelming, and you went ahead and did it anyway? What were the results?

Looking out the indigo window, unworkable ideas can be quickly rejected without too much time being spent considering them, or you can go ahead with your plans, knowing the odds are against you.

IDEA #50 Games using negative information and the Easter story.

In this first game, players must figure out the possible causes of a given situation using only negative information.

Students stand in a circle. The leader tells of a mysterious consequence; for example, "All the candles went out."

Beginning with one student and moving around the circle, each student gives a reasonable explanation. For example, "Someone blew them out." The leader explains a reason why this would be impossible. For example, "No one was in the room."

The next student makes a guess using the information that no one was in the room. For example: "A great wind blew them out."

Each time a sensible reason is given, the leader counters it giving a new clue in a negative form. The new clue always excludes the guess and narrows the range of possibilities.

If a student cannot come up with a reasonable suggestion using all the facts, he or she drops out of the game. There are no right or wrong answers but they must be reasonable ones.

There is *no* correct explanation of the event. The point is to find answers using negative information only. Who can think of the most possibilities?

Now play a biblical game. Using the same rules and procedure as above, give this mysterious consequence: "On Easter morning the tomb was empty." This gives your students a new perspective for considering the Easter story.

After exploring all logical explanations, say: There are events in this life that cannot be explained.

Fact: Focusing on the negative helps planning.

There are times when the negative needs to be before us so that we can understand all angles. Don't let it keep you from pursuing a good plan, but use it to make the plan a better one.

IDEA #51 Plan a rally. Divide the class into groups. Give them these instructions: You are a committee that is planning a peace rally in the city park. Make a list of indigo window things that could go wrong—so that you can plan for contingencies. A good way to get the list going is to instruct each person to say "I see a danger that _____."

Share the lists from the various groups. Where was there overlap? Did one group realize something none of the others could foresee? Write all the negatives on the board.

Now you can plan for alternatives. For example, if it should rain where is an alternative place to hold the rally?

IDEA #52 Again divide into groups to deal with the question, "Why is Sunday school boring?" The negative fact is that children are not coming to Sunday school. Why? Again the groups work on a list of indigo window suggestions and then share with the larger group.

In this case the indigo window is not used to build doubt but is used to point out weaknesses in an objective manner so that we can deal with them and correct them.

IDEA #53 Play "I'll Bet You Can't." This is a fun game that illustrates the concept of focusing on the negative. Though ridiculous at times, it helps students generate creative possibilities from negative suggestions.

How to play:

"It" tells the group something he or she would like to do. For example, "I'd like to fly a helicopter."

Members of the class challenge "It" by naming an object that could not be used to do it. For example, "I'll bet you can't use a pillow to fly a helicopter."

"It" must find a reasonable use for the object. For example, "I could use it to sit on."

If "It" cannot come up with a use for the object, the challenger becomes "It" and chooses an action. The game continues.

IDEA #54 A biblical version of "I'll Bet You Can't."

In this version of the game above, "It" is given a Bible character and situation as the action. The rest of the game continues as above.

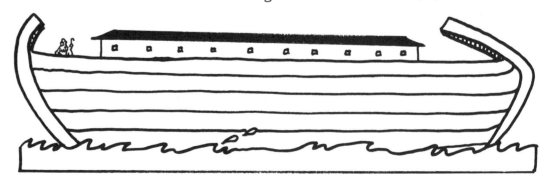

1. You are young David and you are going out to kill Goliath.
2. You are Moses leading the children of Israel through the wilderness.
3. You are Noah building the ark.
4. You are Jonah fleeing from God.
5. You are Daniel in the lions' den.
6. You are Esther trying to save her people.
7. You are the Wise Men traveling to see Jesus.
8. You are the four friends trying to get the paralyzed man through the roof to see Jesus.
9. You are Saul (Paul) on the road to Damascus.
10. You are Paul setting out on your missionary journeys.

These stories include strange objects and actions. To think about: Many and diverse objects and actions and ways are used to bring about God's purpose. Ask the students, What is the strangest thing that God has used in your life? Will you share your story?

Fact: We can deal with "We've never done it that way before."

Sometimes we run into this negative: "We've never done it that way before." If we can put that in the category of indigo window learning it takes the sting out of the statement and we have a better chance to deal with it. We can say, "This proposal does not fit our previous experience." Then we can decide how we want to deal with it.

Jesus often ran into this situation.

IDEA #55 Bible study: Present the case of the woman healed on the Sabbath (Luke 13:10-17).

Instructions: Choose two players. One reads the Old Testament passages Exodus 20:8 and Leviticus 16:31. This player has one minute to present the Pharisees' arguments and to persuade the class that this way of action is best.

Player 2 reads Luke 13:10-17 and has one minute to present Jesus' argument.

The class votes with applause for the stronger argument. Instruct the class not to vote on the "right" answer but to vote for the strongest, best-presented argument.

Fact: The negative can be fun.

IDEA #56 Try cartooning. Cartooning is a fun teaching device. You don't have to be able to draw well. You can just make stick figures and then let them say whatever you want.

Draw a cartoon and come up with an indigo window negative statement by one of the characters.

1. Situation: Peter is telling his wife that he has just decided to follow Jesus. What does she say?
2. Situation: Delilah has just cut off Samson's hair. What does Delilah say? One response I received from a student was, "Samson, I never knew your ears were so big."
3. Situation: Moses has just told Miriam that God has instructed him to lead the children of Israel out of Egypt. What does Miriam say? One response I received: "You? You can't even find your way out of a reed basket."

Use of cartooning illustrates three characteristics of negative thinking:

1. It is easier to be negative than positive.
2. It is more fun to be negative because achievement is immediate and complete.
3. Attacking an idea gives an instant feeling of superiority.

Share the cartoons from the class. Do these three points apply? Do you agree with the three negative aspects of indigo window thinking?

Through humor we may see the destructive aspects of indigo window viewing.

Fact: We can scrutinize the negative.

IDEA #57 Play the game "Beautiful Things."

Read Philippians 4:8.

"It" decides on a beautiful or lovely or good thing and describes it in negative words. For example, a rose can prick you, the petals fall off after a few days, and it has bugs on it.

"It" describes the object as thoroughly as possible using truthful statements but making it sound as unattractive as possible.

The group tries to guess the object. The one who guesses correctly is the next "It," and the game continues.

For discussion:
Do you know people who always emphasize the negative?
How do Paul's words apply to this game?

The power to see the world in a strong, fresh, and beautiful way is a strong, creative force.

IDEA #58 Give each student a piece of clay the size of a walnut. Instruct them to create an ugly object with it. Share these creations.

Now using the same clay turn your piece of clay into something beautiful. Share your new creation. Did you notice that "ugly" things often have no shape or form? They are more like "blobs." As you continue to work, the object begins to take shape and become beautiful.

Read together Genesis 1:1-2.

Does this experience call up a story? A Christian educator shared with me a situation her high school son experienced. His teacher hated the plastic covers he used for reports. She labeled them "ugly" and "babyish." At Christmas the boy took the plastic spines of these covers, cut them in two, heated them until they were pliable, and shaped them into candy canes. He tied a bunch together with a bright ribbon and added the note, "Beauty is in the eye of the beholder." The teacher was delighted with her corsage.

Fact: We can study biblical characters using the negative.

IDEA #59 Judas coin drama.

Step 1: Read Matthew 26:14-16, Mark 14:10-11, and Luke 22:3-6 slowly and prayerfully.

Step 2: Imagine you were there, witnessing this actual experience.

Step 3: Can you carry it a step farther and imagine you are an inanimate object? The Old Testament speaks of stones as being witnesses. Consider what you would witness if you were the coins of silver given to Judas. Consider how important you think the money was to Judas. Was this the reason for his betrayal?

Step 4: Rewrite the scene of Judas' betrayal from the point of view of the coins.

Step 5: If your group is playful create coin costumes by drawing the image of a coin—the front and back—on two large sheets of poster paper. Fasten the two sheets together and wear them as a sandwich board.

Step 6: Speak the lines you have written wearing your coin costumes. What new insights to the story do you get by approaching it from a different perspective?

Step 7: Read Matthew 27:3-10. Imagine another ending. Imagine Judas continuing to live, trying to make up for his terrible mistake. Let the coins speak of ways they could have been used helpfully.

IDEA #60 The guards' coin drama.

Read Matthew 28:11-15. Consider this biblical scene from the point of view of the coins.

Think about the guards at the tomb. They had evidence of the Resurrection yet took money to keep silence. If you knew for certain that someone had come back from the dead could you be paid to keep that quiet? What would be your price? A million dollars? A thousand dollars? A hundred dollars? Ten dollars? Then what would you do with the money?

Use the steps above to create a skit with the guards and the coins.

IDEA #61 Handpainting—story of Thomas.

Thomas is another biblical character we associate with the negative. The indigo window sees what is wrong, incorrect, and in error, what doesn't fit with accepted knowledge. So did Thomas. Read his story, John 20:24-29.

Thomas has come to be known as the doubting disciple, the one who had to be shown before he would believe. He was a realist who thought "seeing is believing."

We will try to experience Thomas' story through handpainting.

Using washable Magic Markers, draw a design in the palm of your hand. Create a symbol or picture of something you believe about God that cannot be seen. For example, if you believe that God is love you might draw a heart in the palm of your hand. If you believe that God created the world, you might draw a world.

Open your hand to show your design to others.

Consider: 1. Do you usually take things at face value?
2. When is doubting constructive?
3. Why is it hard for some people to believe what they have not seen?
4. Are people who doubt usually open to changing their minds?

Both of these men, Judas and Thomas, were selected by Jesus as close disciples. Jesus seemed to recognize a tremendous potential in both of these indigo window gazers. Judas misused his potential, but Thomas used his doubts as a foundation for finding the truth. God has given all of us freedom of choice.

IDEA #62 Study Nicodemus—play "Atlanta/banana."

Nicodemus was a doubting follower of Jesus. Read his story in John 3:1-10.

Nicodemus had questions. He did not understand Jesus. He looked at reality as he knew it, and he looked at the works of Jesus and asked, "How can this be?"

Play the game "Atlanta/banana" to experience what Nicodemus was feeling.

Directions: The leader says, "I am going to Atlanta and I'm going to buy bananas. Where are you going?"

The students try to guess the puzzle. To answer correctly they must name a *city* and a *fruit,* and the fruit must start with a letter that alphabetically follows the starting letter of the city.

Let the students suggest answers. Tell them "no" until they answer correctly. If one student solves the puzzle do not tell the others.

The bewilderment, the not-quite-getting-it, the almost understanding— parallels the feelings Nicodemus was experiencing.

Indigo window teaching tells us we should not strive to superimpose the structure of our own mind, our own system of thought on reality. There is another way of seeing.

Fact: We recall the ugly so that it will not be repeated.

IDEA #63 Celebrate Kristallnacht.

On a trip to the Holy Land, our tour group was taken to the Holocaust Museum. A few persons did not want to go in to see the horrors. Others glanced briefly and then returned to the tour bus. But our guide insisted, "You must see it all, so that you will not forget."

We can reenact as well as recall. A church in Ohio observes "Kristallnacht." Their church members were sent this information: The term "Kristallnacht" (literally, "Night of Crystal") refers to the organized anti-Jewish riots of November 9–10, 1938. These riots marked a fundamental transition in Nazi policy and were a harbinger of the "Final Solution." Ninety-one Jews were killed, 30,000 were deported to concentration camps, 191 synagogues were burned, 7,000 Jewish shops and businesses were looted, and the sacred Torah scrolls were burned and desecrated.

It behooves each of us to remember and to commit ourselves to understanding and appreciating the differences among people. That which we forget, we are doomed to repeat. Only by education and acceptance can we guarantee that a Holocaust will never happen again.

The Jewish community has asked churches to join with synagogues each year in keeping their lights on all night, beginning the evening of November 9 until the morning of the 10th, to remember that the Holocaust began with the sound of shattered glass and ended with the silence of the dead.

Announce the celebration of Kristallnacht in your church bulletin and encourage families to respond. Or, take this on as a Sunday school project.

Remembering the past is dangerous, for it is possible to despair and grow bitter. The challenge is to remember with hope and commitment that the terrible will not be repeated.

Fact: Judgment is followed by grace.

There is judgment in the Bible, but reading or studying about this without also studying grace misses the point of the Good News.

The pointed finger, the raised fist, the bellowing voice, the pronouncements of "must" and "should" all leave us with an unfinished message—

the Crucifixion without the Resurrection. It is always easier to get an audience when we are denouncing something, but in doing so we are leaving out a crucial point. God's word is two-edged—of judgment and grace, and the slant is toward grace.

IDEA #64 A Confederate soldier's prayer.

Augustine said, "God does not ask us to tell Him our needs that He may learn about them but in order that we may be capable of receiving what He is preparing to give."

In the light of this statement, read the following prayer by an anonymous Confederate soldier.

> I asked God for strength, that I might achieve,
> I was made weak, that I might learn humbly to obey.
> I asked for health, that I might do greater things,
> I was given infirmity that I might do better things.
> I asked for riches, that I might be happy,
> I was given poverty, that I might be wise.
> I asked for power, that I might have the praise of men,
> I was given weakness, that I might feel the need of God.
> I asked for all things, that I might enjoy life,
> I was given Life, that I might enjoy all things.
> I got nothing that I asked for—but everything I had hoped for
> Almost despite myself, my unspoken prayers were answered.
> I am, among all men, most richly blessed.

This author used poetry to speak of God's judgment and grace. Ask your students: What method would you use? How would you pass along this idea? With whom would you be willing to share this thought, and what might you expect as their response?

There are at least four things we can do with indigo window thinking:

1. We can accept it as valid reasoning. For example, whales *do* ingest balloons.
2. We can dismiss it as invalid. For example, it is not true that the only way to include children in worship is with a children's sermon.
3. We can acknowledge it but propose an alternative. For example, perhaps in the past teachers have not come to training events, but we can make this one so exciting that they will come.
4. We can acknowledge it but counter with an equally probable forecast. For example, it might rain during our peace rally—but it might not.

When we deal with the indigo window this way, we take out the potential for argument and conflict.

•VISIONS AND DREAMS•
LOOKING OUT THE YELLOW WINDOW

Make your face shine upon your servant,
    and teach me your statutes.
                        —Psalm 119:135

"You shall love the Lord your God with all your heart, and with all your soul, and with all your mind." This is the greatest and first commandment.
                        —Matthew 22:37-38

Dictionary definition
SOUL: *the spiritual part of a person*

INTRODUCTION TO YELLOW WINDOW TEACHING

Our final window is the yellow window. In teaching Sunday school, it is not enough to train critical minds. We are in this business to make things better, to receive and tell the Good News. Thomas a Kempis in *Imitation of Christ* says, "God's mercies to you need a lot of thinking over. At such times put your thirst for knowledge on one side—read so as to soften the heart."

A true religious understanding, besides content knowledge and a loving relationship with God and an inquiring mind, requires an illumination the teacher cannot give. The role of the teacher is to help in the preparation for this experience, which God gives. Our role is to offer pathways so that all who teach and learn in the Spirit might be made new.

Gazing out the yellow window we seek a perception that sparkles with sunshine. We seek a certainty that we are directly in touch with profound depths of reality that are usually hidden. We view this certainty with optimism.

The story is told of Albert Einstein that once he lost his ticket while riding the train to a speaking engagement. He looked in his pockets, opened his suitcases. Finally the ticket agent said, "Don't worry, Dr. Einstein. We know you and trust you. We know you will send us the money." "No, no, you don't understand young man," Einstein said. "The question is not of my honesty. The question is, Where am I going?"

Looking out the yellow window we look for the vision: Where are we going? We look for the big picture, the best possible scenario, the dreams, the vision of what can be.

This is the most important kind of teaching we do in Sunday school, and it is the most difficult to teach in a traditional setting. First we must receive the vision. Then we must be able to communicate the vision, to break open the word of God and let it loose in the world. Every Sunday school lesson should contain some expression of the "Good News" of our faith. Can you locate such an opportunity in your lesson for next Sunday? Mark it with a yellow window.

Receiving this "Good News," we do not wallow in euphoria but look for the demands this places on us.

Another problem with this style of teaching is that it is the most self-revealing about our own faith life. Children particularly are sensitive observers of adults, and they will pick up on our attitudes. The realness and genuineness of our own faith will be unmasked.

Yellow window gazing is looking on the bright side, a deliberate search for the positive—the best possible scenario—the Kingdom come. The yellow window approach is an attitude that moves ahead of the current situation with positive hope. The yellow window defines an opportunity. It is a vision that says, It can be done and it is worth doing.

The excitement and stimulation of a vision go far beyond objective judgment. A vision sets a direction. The Bible says, "Without vision, the people perish."

YELLOW WINDOW APPROACHES

Approach: Seeing the Big Picture.

In cultivating a vision we look first at the big picture. We try to really see life as related, infinite, and purposive. We look for the unity of all things in God.

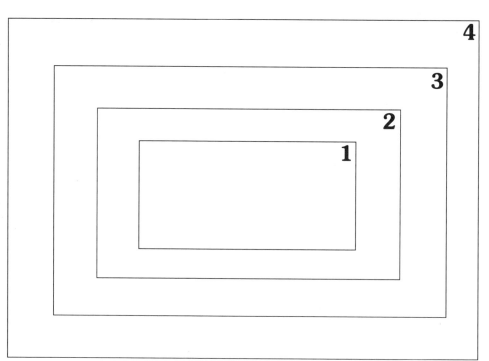

The Big Picture Perspective

IDEA #65 Do a Big Picture exercise.

Give every student a box similar to the one presented on page 72. Tell them that you will read a description and they are to write down their feelings in the appropriate section.

Box 1: I was looking out a hotel window downtown in a large city. The street was deserted except for the one parked truck. Two children came out of an ice-cream store, licking huge ice-cream cones. They started down the sidewalk.
(Give the class time to record their feelings, then continue reading:)

Box 2: Before reaching my hotel the children turned into an alley. Because of the way the light reflected I could see into the alley. It was filled with garbage cans and debris.
(Students write their feelings about the situation now in Box 2.)

Box 3: To my horror I saw a masked man step out from behind one of the cans and approach the children, his arm raised to strike. The truck had started to move.
(Students write their reactions in Box 3.)

Box 4: The truck came closer. I could see a large camera and the name of a motion picture studio. Someone yelled "Take." The bandit took off his mask and the children smiled.
(Students write reactions in Box 4.)

Teacher: Look at your sheet. Look at your feelings recorded in Box 1 and your feelings in Box 4. How different things are when you get the big picture!

Follow this exercise with the biblical Big Picture.

IDEA #66 A biblical big picture.

In our work in the church, we experience burn-out not necessarily because we are overworked but because we are overburdened with the trivial and the unimportant. We forget the big picture.

Give the students another Box and follow the directions above.

Box 1: Jesus is born. Recall all your associations with that birth story. Remember the shepherds, the angels, the wise men. What feelings does this story call up in you?

Box 2: Recall Jesus' ministry. Remember the healings and the miracles, the teaching and the preaching. Remember the hillside at Galilee, the disciples, the crowds that followed him. What feelings do these stories call up?

Box 3: Recall Jesus' death. Remember the stories of the Last Supper, the betrayal, the trial, the crucifixion, the death. Write your feeling words in Box 3.

Box 4: Remember the Resurrection! The empty tomb! The surprised followers! Recall the appearances at Emmaus and by the seaside. Write your feelings.

Look over your page at the big picture of Jesus' life. See how his life unfolded? How does your life parallel this story?

The gospel means "Good News." What is the Good News that God unveils through every stage of Jesus' life? of your life?

It is good news to have the sense of being worthwhile and accepted and blended with God's purpose—just because we exist.

Approach: Your church can have a vision.

Churches are forced to solve problems, but no one is ever forced to look for opportunities. In yellow window gazing we look for opportunities and visions for our local church.

IDEA #67 Draw a vision.

The positive spectrum of the yellow window ranges from visions and dreams to the logical and practical.

Consider with your class: Where are we going as a local church? We pause from our usual hustle and rushing to recall again what we, as a church, are all about.

Great leaders have felt they had a purpose, a mission in life, a destiny. Our visions can be nurtured by studying and musing on the lives of these persons.

Anwar Sadat felt his mission in life was to bring peace to the Middle East. He made an unprecedented visit to Israel to meet with the leaders of the Jewish world.

Recall Martin Luther King, Jr.'s, march to Selma.

Recall Gandhi's march to the Ganges River.

Two characteristics common to these three trips are:

1. Each of these leaders had a vision and cared passionately about its outcome.
2. Each embodied the vision through a dramatic act—a journey.

A vision often starts as the result of an individual's soul searching and then finds expression in a specific act.

Instruct the members of the class to draw a road symbolizing where your church is going. Consider these questions:

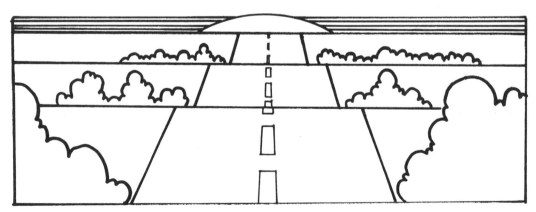

Where would your church march to?
For what purpose?
Who is leading the march?
Who is following?
What is at the end of the road?

Drawing gives us a literal picture of our vision. Share and discuss the pictures.

Pride in our church and enthusiasm for its work must underlie our vision. What steps could you take to bring about this vision?

There is a reaching out and a reaching forward that accompanies visions—a willingness to take great risks.

IDEA #68 Tell your top stories.

Stories are powerful ways to motivate, teach, and spread enthusiasm. We have our wonderful Bible stories, but we also have, in our churches, real-life winners. Do we collect and use these stories?

What is a success story from a member of your class or church?

A recent story from your social outreach?

A story of healing?

A recent story of joy?

Ask your class: What are the three top stories making the rounds in your church today?

Listen to the language used in these stories. Does the language show passionate pride in the church, its mission, and its people?

I asked two different churches for their three top stories and got these responses:

Church 1: We have a mission team going to Haiti.
We had standing room only at our Bell Choir Concert.
Our pastor received an award for her preaching.

Church 2: We are looking for a janitor.
We undersubscribed our budget.
We are trying to locate lost audiovisuals and library books.

Do you get a picture of each of these churches? Of course we do not want to be Pollyannas, always naively optimistic, but we do want to generate vision, energy, and empathy.

I have found that most churches, when asked for their three top stories, include one or more stories about church upkeep. What does this tell us?

Listen to the negative stories too. Don't dismiss them as untrue. The stories may not be factual, but they reveal people's underlying beliefs and doubts. If all your stories are negative, look at the indigo window section for ways to use these negative stories.

The cumulative drift of stories is a good measure of your church's vitality and vision.

IDEA #69 Look at the long haul, using needlepoint.

Yellow window gazing not only sees the vision but incorporates a desire to make things happen. We look ahead and speculate on what might happen. The key here is to look for the action that follows the optimism.

Ask: Where will our church be five years from now?
What is worth doing for a long period of time?
On what do we want to expend time and energy?

Recall Bible stories that keep moving toward a dream over a long period of time. We probably think first of Moses and the forty years in the wilderness. Remember also Joseph in the land of Egypt with the seven years of plenty and the seven years of famine. What other Bible stories come to your mind?

We can never be as certain about the future as we are about the past. We set out to do something because it is worth doing. But it is hard to be patient over the long haul. We want results and we want them *now*.

Bishop Desmond Tutu told this story at the World Methodist Conference in Kenya in 1986: "Once upon a time the black people owned the land of South Africa, and then minerals and ores were discovered and the white man came. He brought with him a little black book. He said, 'Come learn about this book and this God and pray.' And we came and prayed and when we opened our eyes—we had the book and the white man had the land."

"Ah. But," Bishop Tutu said, "the thing is—We got the best part of the bargain." Then he read Isaiah 11:4-9 and said, "This is what we believe. We shall be free. About that there can be no doubt. The black cause of liberation will triumph, must triumph because it is a just and righteous cause. God is on our side because He is always on the side of the oppressed. Some of us will die. It does not matter. God is working His purpose out."

Willingness to wait and work and suffer—over the long haul.

Can we affirm that God is indeed working his purpose out in God's time and in God's way?

To experience this, work on a long-range craft project with your class. Needlepoint works well. Select a beautiful Christian symbol with deep colors.

Week after week, work on the seemingly endless tiny stitches that fill in the background. Have the work on hand for those who come to class early. This year's class may not even finish it.

If needlepoint is impractical in your situation, consider making a linoleum block print or a multi-colored silk-screen or any project that takes time to create. Discuss, as you work, how we can bring about God's kingdom—little by little, small thing by small thing, working steadily—over the long haul.

Eventually the finished work appears, and if our work is careful, it is very beautiful.

Our Christian heritage affirms again and again how impractical visions and dreams pursued over the long haul eventually make those dreams a reality.

Approach: We study biblical visions.

Biblical persons experienced profound inner transformation that brought their wills into conformity with God's purposes.

IDEA #70 Embody visionary characteristics.

Step 1: Read I Kings 19:11. God said "Go out and stand on the mountain before the Lord, for the Lord is about to pass by."
Continue reading through verse 13.

Step 2: Try to imagine this scene in your mind. Imagine Elijah's experience of a windstorm, an earthquake, and a fire. Then imagine God's voice speaking after the fire in a sound of sheer silence.

Step 3: Read about another encounter with God. Acts 9:1-9. Pause and contemplate verses 5-6: "I am Jesus, whom you are persecuting. But get up and enter the city, and you will be told what you are to do."

Step 4: Imagine Paul's experience. God spoke through a blinding light and the voice of Jesus. Think about these overwhelming experiences given at unexpected times.

We study these experiences. We tell these stories. We give validity to these experiences. We affirm that this is our tradition and heritage, and we do not deny the possibility of this happening again.

It would be helpful simply to role-play these two great Bible stories, but to experience the stories more deeply, try this:

Divide the class into four sections. Name the following four characteristics exemplified in the biblical experiences we have just read about.

Courage
Acceptance
Power
Joy

Each group is to create a living sculpture personifying these characteristics. Each student in each group positions his or her body to illustrate the assigned characteristic.

The teacher may ask: How do you show courage with your body? How would you stand? Feet firmly planted? Shoulders back?

How can our bodies personify acceptance? Reaching out? Up? Where would you be looking?

How do arms and legs and posture show power?
What is the stance of joy?

Give the groups time to discuss and practice these postures.

Now connect the individual statues so that all persons in each group are touching someone. The result is four large living sculptures personifying a characteristic of someone receiving a vision.

Study the group statues for understanding. We can learn from our bodies. The excitement and stimulation of a great vision can be experienced in our lives.

Physically sense what cannot be defined. What we are seeking to teach is this: Expect revelation and do not fear it!

A mystical experience cannot be scheduled or forced, but we can make our students aware of the possibility and encourage them to welcome it when it comes!

IDEA #71 Recall other biblical dreams and visions.

Someone has said, "Stories are the oldest form of remembering the promises we made to God and that God made to us."

The stories of our faith are a strong positive heritage we give our children. They help us generalize and interpret our experiences of following out our dreams. Stories are alive. They call forth a response from us.

Step 1: Divide the class into three groups. Assign two of the following Bible stories to each group:
1. The Resurrection of Jesus. (Mark 16:1-8)
2. Moses sees the Promised Land. (Deut. 34:1-8)
3. Joshua captures Jericho. (Josh. 5:13–6:27)
4. David defeats Goliath. (I Sam. 17:1-51)
5. Sarah has a baby. (Gen. 21:1-7)
6. Elijah defeats the prophets of Baal. (I Kings 18:20-38)

Step 2: After each group reads the assigned stories, the group should rate them on the likelihood of their happening, using the chart below:

_____ Very likely, based on experience

_____ Good chance

_____ Even chance

_____ No better than possible

_____ Remote or long shot

_____ No way

Step 3: Do these stories call up a story of their own? In the small groups, share personal stories of winning against overwhelming odds.

Step 4: Bring the three groups together for sharing.

Step 5: Close by saying, "A vision has been defined as a goal there is little hope of reaching." What do these stories of our faith say to this definition?

Approach: We have personal visions.

Yellow window gazing is a deliberate search for the positive. Where is the "Good News" in your individual life?

The fuel that supplies us is the conviction that what we do has meaning. Our lives have meaning. When we no longer find meaning in what we do even the smallest actions drain us.

IDEA #72 Symbolize your faith.

(Used with permission from The Center for Research in Faith and Moral Development and Father Paul Johnson, O.P.):

—Jot down answers beside each question below.
—Then, on a separate sheet of paper, draw a picture or symbol that expresses your understanding of God at these points of your life.

My Childhood Image of God

	What was going on in your life? What was important to you and gave your life meaning? What was faith to you?

My Adolescent Image of God

	What was going on in your life? What was important to you and gave your life meaning? What was faith to you?

My Present Image of God

	What is going on in your life? What is important to you and gives your life meaning? What is faith to you?

How My Image of God Might Change

	What in your life is calling forth this new image of God?

Visions and
Dreams/
Looking
Out the
Yellow Window

79

1. Study your picture and questions alone or with others for *purpose*. Is there some clarification of purpose that runs as a strand through our life?

   With so much second-hand *experience* in our lives (from T.V., computers, etc.), people are experiencing a profound sense of an unlived life. Many long for an explosion into vividness and meaning.

2. Study your picture for *faith development*. Is there clarification of your personal faith growth? What do you sense? Faith points to a mysterious and unordinary dimension that is always beyond or something more than argument and evidence.

3. Study your pictures for *values*. Do you discover any illumination of values in your life as you look at these pictures and ponder these questions?

If the holy comes into the world wherever humans let it in, perhaps even our lives are, after all, fertile ground for experiences of the sacred.

IDEA #73 Value clarification prayer.

Complete the statements below. You may write one sentence or a whole paragraph. Write "nothing" for any sentence for which you have no answer, or "pass" if you'd prefer not to say.

1. I would be willing to die for _____.
2. I would be willing to physically fight for _____.
3. I would argue strongly in favor of _____.
4. I would quietly take a position in favor of _____.
5. I will share only with my friends my belief that _____.
6. I prefer to keep to myself my belief that _____.

Meditate on Galatians 3:3-5: "You began by God's Spirit; do you now want to finish by your own power?" (GNB). Write a prayer inspired by this meditation. Include your values charted above. We are looking for depth of meaning that satisfies the soul.

We orient ourselves. We open ourselves through daily attention to prayer, meditation, and ministry to that which is greater than ourselves.

Perhaps our prayer is for the deepening of beliefs already held, for strength and courage to live out our convictions.

Approach: Music creates vision.

Nothing has quite the power to inspire us that music has. The news is so good, mere words fail us. We must sing and shout and dance.

IDEA #74 Set your vision and illuminate your way with a hymnfest.

The concept of a hymnfest is Welsh in origin. It is a meaningful way to teach vision and inspiration as an entire congregation comes together for an hour of singing.

Individual Sunday school classes could offer special hymns, and the congregational singing could be varied by including handbells, brass ensembles, and special instruments such as a flute or timpani.

Some visionary hymns and ways of singing are suggested below. Choose those which are most meaningful to your particular church.

Hymnfest

Leader: Rejoice in the Lord, you righteous;
it is good for the just to sing praises.
All: We lift our voices and send our song to you.
Leader: Praise the Lord with the harp;
play to him upon the psaltery and lyre.
All: We lift our voices and send our song to you.
Leader: Sing for God a new song.
Sound a fanfare with all your skill upon the trumpet.
All: We lift our voices and send our song to you.

1. "It Is Well with My Soul"
   verse 1—all
   verse 2—male solo
   verse 3—female solo
   verse 4—all
2. "Be Thou My Vision"
   verses 1 and 2—youth in unison,
   a verse with bells only
   verse 3—all in unison
3. "This Little Light of Mine"
   children's Sunday school class
4. "Let There Be Peace on Earth"
   entire congregation with brass accompaniment
5. "Where He Leads Me"
   entire congregation in harmony with piano accompaniment
6. "Jesus, Joy of Our Desiring"
   verse 1—Soloist sings a phrase and the congregation echoes back.
   verse 2—all in unison
7. "All Things Bright and Beautiful"
   stanza by all
   children only on each refrain
8. "Hymn of Promise"
   verse 1—all
   verse 2—all with flute accompaniment
   verse 3—all
9. "Amazing Grace"
   verse 1—all
   verse 2—women
   verse 3—men
   verses 4 and 5—choir
   verse 6—all
10. "All Hail the Power of Jesus' Name"
    All sing all verses with timpani accompaniment

Visions and
Dreams/
Looking
Out the
Yellow Window

Approach: We affirm Sunday school.

Setting out to look at something in a positive way may itself create a new perception. There is value in affirming our values.

IDEA #75 Build a modular tower.

Give the class time to think of all the positive attributes of Sunday school that they can. Have on hand a large supply of boxes in all shapes and sizes, as well as picture magazines, scissors, and felt-tipped markers.

Step 1: Cover the boxes with yellow construction paper, or paint them yellow.
Step 2: On each box write an attribute of the Sunday school in bold black letters, or paste on a picture to express the attribute.
Step 3: Pile the boxes on top of one another into a modular tower; then stand back and look at it. The juxtaposition of images in strange and bizarre ways sparks insight.
Step 4: March around the tower singing "We're Marching to Zion."
Step 5: Say together, in affirmation, the words from Joshua 24:14-15: "Now therefore revere the Lord, and serve him in sincerity and in faithfulness; put away the gods that your ancestors served beyond the River and in Egypt, and serve the Lord. Now if you are unwilling to serve the Lord, choose this day whom you will serve . . . but as for me and my household, we will serve the Lord."
Step 6: Create a cheer with movements for the last phrase.

Approach: God speaks through dreams.

The Scriptures are full of dreams and stories of God speaking to persons through dreams. Consider the provocative words of Isaiah 45:3: "I will give you the treasures of darkness/and riches hidden in secret places,/so that you may know that it is I, the Lord,/the God of Israel, who call you by your name."

IDEA #76 Make pictures on a sand table.

Sand seems to be a good medium for dreams. There is the same sifting, fleeting quality. We associate sand with sand castles by the sea, with a tactile kind of learning that defies definition.

You don't see sand tables much in Sunday school any more. Years ago this was a Sunday school staple. If you have access to one, try this:

Seek to re-create, on a sand table, dream experiences from the Bible.

Give each student a place at the sand table. As you read a dream story from the Bible, each student draws the story in the sand with a stick or a finger.

Before beginning say: "When we hear a story our mind forms inner pictures. We bring to bear all our past experiences that relate to the story. For this reason no two persons hear a story in exactly the same way. We will create in the sand the picture we see in our minds—the image we have—and then we will share our pictures with one another."

Use these Bible stories:
Samuel called by God while he was sleeping (I Sam. 3:1-18)
Joseph whose future was foretold in dreams (Gen. 37:5-11)
Jacob who dreamed of angels (Gen. 28:10-17)

After each story, share the pictures. Then erase the sand pictures and go on to the next dream story.

Talk with your class about the feelings in dreams: indefinable, puzzling, odd, fuzzy, vague. Remember together how dreams fit things together in odd combinations—sometimes funny, sometimes frightening, mostly just strange.

Let the children share a recent dream. Talk together about the difficulty of recalling dreams—how by focusing we try to recall something vague. It's there but we can't call it up. Dreams are the unconscious part of our experiences.

For these Bible characters, insight came from dreams—a moment of discovery. There was an archetypal understanding—a willingness to know things in their deepest, most mythic sense as treasures from dark, secret places.

Consider prayerfully the words read earlier from I Samuel 3:1: "The word of the Lord was rare in those days; visions were not widespread."

Pray for visions and understanding.

IDEA #77 Daydream poetry.

Daydreams are a special form of thinking. They usually involve mental images, pictures in the mind's eye, caused by something on our minds. Daydreams offer hopes, things to look forward to.

Poetry is a good medium to call up and make concrete our daydreams.

Step 1: Ask your class to daydream about their wishes. Children are great makers of wishes.

Step 2: Ask them to stretch their imaginations and complete this sentence:
I wish _____.
Ask them to try to present a vivid picture in their writing.

Step 3: Then, invite the students to look at their wish. Is it self-centered? Whom would it help? Would the world be a better place if you received your wish? Whom would it hurt?

Step 4: Share the wishes. Write them all on the board. The result is a kind of vicarious experience. We enter into one another's daydreams.

Combine the wishes into a collaborated poem. We can shape and guide our daydreams into constructive thinking.

Step 5: Share this thought with your class: If you can dream it—you can do it. Pretend there is a T.V. in your head. See yourself carrying out your daydream, saying and doing the right thing to bring it about. We have the ability to take on the shapes of our own dreams!

In this experience, "teaching" is not really the right word. It is more like permitting children to discover something they already have—their dreams.

Summary

To summarize what we have been saying, teaching in the Sunday school is a creative act. It calls forth special gifts and is a constant search for new and relevant ways to tell the old story.

Our teaching in the Sunday school is enriched if we understand what it is we are trying to teach and the methods that work best in each instance. We classify learning and seek appropriate techniques.

We use the image of a colored window to indicate to us as teachers and to our class the type of teaching and learning we are experiencing.

The white window is for seeing all the neutral facts that broaden our understanding of the Bible and our Christian faith. We search for and try out all methods that can present neutral facts. Some are listed in the white window section. There are many others. We did not mention map study or crossword puzzles, or all sorts of quizzes and fact-finding games. The list goes on and on. The focus is facts.

The red window addresses our emotions—the whole area of feelings. Here our methods are subjective, personal, yet touching on universal feelings. We seek to bring these feelings to the surface in our classroom through art and drama and play and movement. We accept our feelings as what it is to be human, and we ponder how best to channel these powerful aspects of learning. We seek to grow toward God through our feelings.

The indigo window accepts the negative part of our personality—a combination of negative facts and feelings. In our classrooms, we affirm the doubt, the questioning, even the despair, that constitute a genuine search for God. We use Bible study to probe, not so much for answers, as for understanding of how others dealt with their doubt. We use games to lighten the oppressiveness of the negative.

The yellow window seeks to illuminate our teaching. Rather than center on methods, we seek to create a happening. We use approaches to teaching and learning that have as their objective the breaking through of God into the lives of our students, the coming of a vision. We realize that there is far more to our relationship with God than we know intellectually.

We dare to be creative—co-creators with God.

These windows seek to illustrate at least four of the avenues of creativity that we as teachers can travel. We also do the following:

1. We identify just what it is we are trying to teach.
2. We choose the most creative way we can to teach it.
3. As creative persons, using our unique gifts, we reach into the depths and bring forth something genuine. We are not distracted by what others are doing. God does not call us all to do the same thing. Our response is individual.
4. We affirm the methods that work best for us as teachers, but try other approaches too, knowing we are enriched by using a variety of windows.

5. In any approach we choose, creativity is not enough. We study and prepare.

What could ever be more exciting than catching a glimpse of God? There are many ways. We seek the view from many windows. How can we be bored as we teach and eagerly watch?

AGE-LEVEL INDEX

The following is a suggested age-level index. Many of the ideas can be used interchangeably with other ages. Please use this index as a guide only, because students' abilities, backgrounds, and interests may be different. Be creative in mixing and matching ideas and age levels.

Age 2 Years
Idea 1. spelling
2. singing
3. searching
4. worship center
5. pictures
6. stories
7. singing again

Ages 3 and 4
Idea 8. memorize
9. display
10. visit
11. musical game
12. echo reading
43. happy faces

Ages 5–7
Idea 13. Bible game
14. sing
15. erase reading
16. rhythm facts
17. Who am I?
45. list poem
76. sand table dreams

Ages 8–10
Idea 18. Bible game
19. true or false
20. multiple choice
21. Bible race
34. writing and pondering
35. Moses story
36. boiling water
38. storytelling drama
41. texture and sounds
42. Jesu rhythmic movements
44. sparklers
45. list poem

54. I'll Bet You Can't
58. ugly object
59. Judas coin drama
75. modular tower
77. daydream poetry

Ages 10–12
Idea 22. guess a person in one sentence
23. string-across
24. advanced string-across
25. headlines
26. Which Came First?
27. number 40 game
28. secret code
37. Kabuki faces
39. Pentecost legend
40. body movements
46. creative writing
50. negative information game
57. beautiful things
61. study Thomas
69. long haul—needlepoint
71. dreams and visions
73. value clarification prayer

Youth and Young Adults
Idea 24. advanced string-across
29. be a reporter
30. report a legal question
31. compare Bible stories
32. true or false
33. write a rap
39. Pentecost legend
40. body movements
48. Daniel report
49. hidden errors
51. plan a rally